ADVICE TO THE SERIOUS SEEKER

ADVICE TO THE SERIOUS SEEKER

Meditations on the Teaching of Frithjof Schuon

James S. Cutsinger

SUNY Series in
Western Esoteric Traditions
David Appelbaum, Editor

STATE UNIVERSITY OF NEW YORK PRESS

Frontispiece: photo of Frithjof Schuon courtesy Whitall N. Perry

Production by Ruth Fisher
Marketing by Nancy Farrell

Published by
State University of New York Press, Albany

For information, address State University of New York Press,
90 State Street, Suite 700, Albany NY 12207

Library of Congress Cataloging-in-Publication Data

Cutsinger, James S., 1953–
    Advice to the serious seeker : meditations on the teaching of
Frithjof Schuon / James S. Cutsinger.
       p.   cm. — (SUNY series in Western esoteric traditions)
     ISBN 0–7914–3249–1 (hardcover : alk. paper). — ISBN 0–7914–3250–5
(pbk. : alk. paper)
      1. Spiritual life—Meditations. 2. Schuon, Frithjof, 1907– .
3. Religions. 4. Religion.   I. Title. II. Series.
BL624.2.C87 1997
200'.92—dc20   96-12876
                                             CIP

10 9 8 7 6 5 4 3 2 1

**To
the Friends**

Blessed is the man who has found Wisdom. Her ways are good ways, and all Her paths are peaceful. She is a tree of life to all that lay hold upon Her.

—Proverbs 3

CONTENTS

Beauty

Prayer

PREFACE

*A*s a professor of religion, I am sometimes asked by students for spiritual advice. This book has been written with such requests in mind. Some of the questions have come from skeptics and cynics, others from those who are attracted to the various new age religious movements. Many have been posed by conservative Christians. I have tried to keep all three groups in mind and to write in such a way that all might profit.

In response to the serious inquirer, I often point to a body of traditional wisdom known as the perennial philosophy, and above all to its leading contemporary expositor, Frithjof Schuon. This book is an attempt to sum up Schuon's teaching on the spiritual life.

My interest in the perennial philosophy is a puzzle to many of my academic colleagues in religious studies, and it has occasionally been a cause for concern among my fellow Orthodox Christians. According to the former, the perennialists are too dogmatic, too insistent upon the importance of traditional religious frameworks, and thus too conservative. In the view of the latter, the perennial philosophy appears not to do justice to the exclusive claims of Christ, and thus it seems too liberal.

I do not expect that these meditations will convert either party, nor in the case of my fellow Christians is that even desirable. But I do hope all my readers might see that there are jewels of Truth here which those of us living at this eleventh hour can ill afford to ignore, and that "far from diminishing a participation in the treasures of the historical Redemption," the perennial philosophy "confers on them a compass that touches the very roots of Existence." I should add in any case Schuon's own proviso: "We do not seek to convert anyone who is at peace with God, if he is so really."

Many friends have helped to make this a better book. I owe a word of special appreciation, however, to Michael Pollack and Michael Fitzgerald, for without their assistance there would have been no book at all. I am also much indebted to Catherine Schuon for her extraordinary generosity and encouragement, to Steven Boyer, Deborah Casey, Marie Hansen, Barry McDonald, Terry Moore, and Scott Murray for numerous helpful suggestions on various drafts of the manuscript, and to Mark Mancuso for his meticulous corroboration of the many quotations and sources. Loving thanks also to my wife, Carol, not only for assistance in proofreading, but for the faithful support and good humor she brings to all my work.

Finally, I want to express my deep and lasting gratitude to my godfather, Alvin Moore, Jr., for his many kindnesses, advice, and wise counsel. Had it not been for him and the doors he opened, I could never have written this book. May God grant him many years.

The publisher requests that a note be inserted concerning my generic use of the word *man* in what follows. As an academic, I am of course well aware of current pressures to conform to the strictures of inclusive language. Nevertheless I remain opposed to this fashion for both philosophical and philological reasons. An ideological manipulation of time-honored meaning seems especially disproportionate in the present series of reflections, which are designed in part to remind the reader of the irreplaceable values of tradition. The editors have kindly agreed to honor my views.

INTRODUCTION:
LANDMARKS ON THE ROAD AHEAD

*Y*ou have asked for my advice about the spiritual life, and I can tell from how the question was posed that you are not going to settle for a glib response. Only the Truth, the whole Truth, and nothing but the Truth will do. While mere complexity of detail is no solution either, of course, a satisfactory answer will need to be large enough, rich enough, to speak at once and with power to both the skeptics and the serious aspirant: both to those around us who doubt whether there is a God at all, and to the one within us who understands in advance that there must be a God, and who longs for His wisdom and likeness.

An acceptable answer must do something else, too. It must provide perspective and be of help in sorting through the bewildering multitude of competing alternatives now available to the spiritual seeker. Which are true and which false? What is efficacious, what is useless, and what is actually dangerous? To judge wisely in such matters requires an understanding of both theory and practice, both doctrine and method. At the very least, therefore, you are going to need not only a map of where you wish to go, but instructions on how to secure food and other provisions for the journey itself. In fact, the complexity and confusion of our day mean that even more is required. More than a map, you will need some lessons in cartography, and more than just food, you need the facts of nutrition. Only then can you know that what you are told is the Truth.

1

Other more specific needs and questions will come to mind as we proceed, but please notice that your order is a tall one already. In fact it is much too tall for the likes of me, and you should understand from the outset that I cannot myself fill it. This is no joke, no rhetorical strategy, no mere show of modesty. I mean what I say. The question you have asked can be properly and effectively answered only by a spiritual master. I do not mean to dismiss the encouragement and prayers of a fellow pilgrim, nor is the practical experience of life to be belittled. Nor again should we ignore the importance of destiny. God has placed you there and me here, and the fact that He has brought us together through your question cannot but mean something. But at the same time I want you to realize that while I shall gladly offer my support as a spiritual friend, I can claim to have no wisdom of my own. All I can do is to pass along what I have received.

I propose to describe for you a teaching that has been of immeasurable help to me personally in coming to grips with the essentials of the spiritual life. This teaching can be described as metaphysical, esoteric, traditional, and perennial. As perhaps you know, each of these terms is laden with a variety of connotations and can be used in several, sometimes mutually exclusive, ways by different philosophical and religious schools of thought. It is most important, therefore, that we begin trying to understand precisely what are, and what are not, the meanings intended in the discussions that follow. By pausing here to offer some preliminary definitions of these important words, I hope to provide an initial sense of the territory that we are going to be exploring.

The word *metaphysical* pertains to God's transcendence. It means very simply that God in Himself cannot be limited. To be precise, metaphysics is the science of the real as such, no matter the dimension we might wish to consider. For the sake of simplicity, however, and in light of the word's etymology, the adjective is here meant to remind us that God is beyond the domain of change and becoming. God exceeds or surpasses not only the tangible boundaries which circumscribe physical objects, and not only the temporal alterations to which they are subject, but the logical limits presupposed in everything susceptible to conceptual form and definition. And yet paradoxically this very same God, precisely because He cannot be limited, cannot be excluded. To see why is to have grasped the key to all that follows. Nothing can bar God's entry into our world—neither space, time, or any of the other "conditions of existence" understood as containers, nor any of their particular, innumerable contents. God is therefore inevitably present within all things, and He can be discovered by an insight which pierces through the outward shells of those things to their hidden kernel. Here is where the word *esoteric* comes in. It refers to what is essential, inward, and intrinsic, whether in an object, a doctrine, or a sacred text, and it describes a method of investigation and a mode of interpretation which seek to find God at the center or heart of forms. Once again I am prescinding from a somewhat wider sense of the word, in which pure esoterism or "esoterism as such" may be equated with metaphysics. Understood for the moment, however, simply in terms of its reference to whatever is inward, the esoteric pertains primarily to the immanence of God. The metaphysical and the esoteric can thus be seen as complementary opposites.

The other two terms have a similar relationship. First, *traditional*. I have said that nothing can resist God's entry. Being infinite, He cannot but enter space, and the force or impact of this entry results in a kind of radiation or reverberation through time. The former can be pictured as a vertical descent, like dropping a stone into a pool of water, while the latter corresponds to centrifugal ripples moving horizontally toward the shore. These ripples are an image of tradition. Tradition is the name we shall give to all that extends and recalls the revelatory entry of God into our world. The image is helpful for another reason, too. The concentric waves in the pool necessarily have a very particular center. They would not have taken their specific shape nor have begun to move along certain definite radii were it not for the center established by the stone's initial impact. Something of the center remains in the waves. It is the same with tradition and traditional teachings. They cannot be just anything. Not to be confused with mere custom or habit, they are strictly dependent upon the specificity and uniqueness of the initial revelation which they are designed to transmit. These teachings are therefore obliged to honor certain formal conditions and constraints on pain of losing contact with their Divine inception.

If you are beginning to think that the esoteric and the traditional are in a certain sense at odds with each other, you are right. Indeed there are some people who would call themselves esoterists—or esotericists—who reject the idea of tradition on the grounds that it accords too much authority to established forms: particular symbols, laws, precepts, and norms. Only by rejecting all such forms, they say, can God be found within. On the other hand, there are traditional-ists—we might also call them exoterists—who reject the idea of the esoteric, and this on the grounds that the inward is at best a distrac-tion, and at worst a dangerous deviation, from what God has unam-biguously made known to all men. According to the perspective we shall be exploring here, each of these groups is right in one respect and wrong in another, for the esoteric and the traditional belong together, whatever the tension or uneasiness at times between them. The reason is simply that there is no inside without an outside, and there is no outside without an inside. It will be necessary to return to this fundamental reciprocity many times.

Finally, let me say something about the word *perennial*. We shall not have occasion to examine this idea directly until the Epilogue, but it will be implicit throughout our discussions. I have already hinted that the perennial and the traditional, like the metaphysical and the esoteric, can be regarded as both opposites and comple-ments. From another point of view, the perennial is a kind of bridge between the traditional and the esoteric. Or yet again, it can be understood as expressing the relationship between God and time, even as the esoteric expresses the relationship between God and space.

God, I have said, is beyond both space and time. His transcen-dence of space results paradoxically in His inward, esoteric presence in all things in space. On the other hand, His transcendence of time results by a corresponding paradox in His being present at all points of time. Like a perennial flower, which blooms every year, God repeatedly springs forth in our world, for no single moment can hold Him, just as no particular form can exhaust Him. This is not to say that the moments are interchangeable or that the forms are equiva-lent. Each form is unique just as each moment is unrepeatable, and in some of these forms and moments, God has revealed Himself more fully and powerfully than in others. On the other hand, our recogni-tion that nothing can limit or enclose God obliges us to conclude that no single point or form can alone be the true one. His metaphysical being has given rise instead to a multiplicity of traditions on the plane of limitation and becoming, each beginning with a Divine descent.

Do remember that we have just started to survey the field before actually setting out on our journey. It is to be expected that this brief and rather elliptical introduction should give rise to new questions, and not the least of these will concern this last point about the perennial repetition of Divine revelation. This is an idea which is bound to prove unacceptable both to esoterists who reject tradition and to traditionalists who are suspicious of esoterism. To suppose that inward Truth has nothing essential to do with outward form, as do the former, is to dismiss the importance of tradition as such, and therefore of all traditions. To suppose on the contrary that outward form and inward Truth are identical, as do the latter, is to insist on one's own form and reject all the others.

But both of these positions belie the nature of God. The middle ground alone is justified. It alone understands why God in his transcendence cannot but be immanent, and why God in His immanence cannot but transcend—why the Truth must take form, but why no form can exhaust the Truth. Ringing the many changes on these fundamental axioms will occupy us for some time. Once we have learned to recognize the many tones they give rise to, and have begun to appreciate the resulting harmonies, we shall circle back in the Epilogue to consider more fully the perennial dimension of the perspective at hand.

The spiritual teaching I am planning to describe is marked by all four of the characteristics just outlined. It is metaphysical, esoteric, traditional, and perennial. It begins with the fact that God is beyond all restriction and form. It provokes our perception of His presence within things. It insists that our relationship with God depends upon His initiative and must be based on a foundation that He has established. And it assumes that several such traditional foundations have been willed by God, and that these are the world's great religions.

I have admitted that I am without any wisdom of my own and that I shall need some assistance in adequately addressing your question. I am myself no master, but what I can do is to point you to the teaching of someone whom I believe to be one of the great spiritual authorities of our time. This teacher is at once a metaphysician, an esoterist, a traditionalist, and a perennialist, and he is the author of many books on the spiritual life. His name is Frithjof Schuon, and he has been called the greatest living exponent of the *philosophia perennis* or perennial philosophy, a perspective also frequently associated with the names of René Guénon and Ananda Coomaraswamy. (Suggested readings by these and other like-minded authors may be found at the end of this book.)

As you will see very shortly, Schuon is no mere scholar, though the breadth of his knowledge in such domains as philosophy, theology, and comparative religion rivals that of almost any academic I know. More important, however, is the depth of his work, which unfailingly cuts straight to the heart of what should concern us all most: our relationship with God. At the same time, it is a very practical, real-istic message, based—in a phrase he often uses—on "the nature of things." Though he calls us to live "in the face of the Absolute," Schuon knows well that we are creatures and that we have certain rights to relativity on "the human margin."

You will find that there is a distinctive texture or tone to Schuon's writing which itself mirrors his focus on essentials. The style is unmistakable and seems connected somehow, as if organically, to the realities he describes. One knows at a glance that a certain passage cannot but have come from Frithjof Schuon. Nor is this fact without bearing on his teaching. He has pointed out that in our day "ideas no longer bite into the intelligence, which slides over concepts without taking time really to grasp them," and he means if possible to break through this triviality and indifference. He also knows that "Truth must be enunciated, not only with a sense of proportion, but also according to a certain rhythm," and it is accordingly with a poet's craftsmanship that he has designed his prose to attract our atten-tion but without enclosing or restricting it.

Schuon is known in many circles for two things primarily: on the one hand, for the perennialism that has been touched on already—for the idea, to use his own formulation, that there is a "transcendent unity of religions"—and, on the other hand, for his criticism of the modern world, for an uncompromising insistence that we are living at a time of unprecedented intellectual, spiritual, and moral deca-dence, corresponding to the *Kali Yuga* or Dark Age of Hindu doctrine. Neither of these more or less extrinsic assertions will be our focus here, however. Those who come looking to quarrel with these aspects of his teaching will undoubtedly go away unpersuaded. But one can-not do everything at once, and it seemed to me that the needs of a serious seeker could be met more directly if he were introduced first to Schuon's spiritual counsel. This is not to say that we should ignore the increasingly important questions posed by religious pluralism. Nor should we forget that the spiritual life includes an ability to dis-cern the signs of the times. My plan in this case, however, is to con-centrate on the essential ingredients or constitutive elements of what Schuon has called the "religion of the heart." These are the intrinsic dimensions of the spiritual life, found in some form in every integral religious tradition. They are the conditions without which no effective approach to God is possible. All of us can profit from a clearer understanding of these conditions, whatever our views of other religions.

There are four such dimensions, each presupposing man's formal or sacramental attachment to a living tradition, and I shall invite you to consider each of them with me in turn. They are Truth, Virtue, Beauty, and Prayer. I pointed out earlier that spirituality comprises both theory and practice, or doctrine and method. Truth is the theoretical or doctrinal dimension of the spiritual path, while Virtue, Beauty, and Prayer pertain in various ways to practice or method. Truth consists in the comprehension of God. Virtue has to do with our conformation to God. Beauty may be called the configuration of God. And Prayer is a matter of concentration on God. We could make the point in yet another way by saying that the spiritual life depends upon doctrine, morality, aesthetics, and spiritual technique.

As we consider the perennial philosophy under each of these headings, you might wish to keep a picture in mind. God, who is Truth, is at one and the same time both our origin and our goal. The Truth must come at the start of the path, but it is also waiting at the end. The path itself passes through a space or field constituted on the one hand by Virtue and on the other by Beauty. And our motion or progress along the path is Prayer. "Metaphysical truth, a life of prayer, moral conformity, interiorizing beauty: this is the essential, and this is our message."

Finally, a word or two about my mode of presentation. I want to do everything I can to make my response to your request as direct, as concrete, and as practical as possible. This is no time to be concerned about footnotes and other scholarly regularities, and I see no point in having to attach a *Schuon says* to everything that comes from his pen. What you need most is to be brought into immediate contact with the treasures of traditional wisdom—without unnecessary detours and without my commentary taking center stage. It is also important that in helping you explore the four essentials, I avoid giving the impression that Schuon's message is expounded in the form of a system. Systematic qualities or aspects can be found within it, but never to the detriment of a certain musical character, and I would like to highlight this music as much as possible.

My solution takes the form of a series of meditations on aphorisms drawn from Schuon's writings. This procedure reflects the "discontinuous" and "quite evidently inexhaustible" quality of his expositions while allowing us to consider them in a more contemplative way, comparable to a meditative stroll in a garden. As we ponder together the meaning of these aphorisms, I shall be making additional use of other passages from Schuon's books, so that he is given the opportunity of commenting as it were on himself. All such borrowings will be indicated by the appropriate marks. You may turn to the Sources of Quotations at the end of the book for directions on tracking down these passages, and the aphorisms, in Schuon himself.

Truth

There is no right superior to that of Truth.

—*The Maharajas of Benares*

❖ Chapter 1 ❖

The Way of Knowledge

Knowledge is one and indivisible.

*I*n setting out on the spiritual journey, it is important to know that a choice presents itself even before we take our first step. Of course from a certain point of view the choice will have been made already by our destiny—by our temperament, by the time and place in which we live, and by other factors beyond our immediate control. It would be a mistake to suppose that the spiritual life is purely a matter of individual preference. As we shall see, there is nothing haphazard or arbitrary about our return to God. Nevertheless, within the framework of possibilities that he is given, a person is always free to select between real alternatives, and that selection will have eternal repercussions.

When I speak of choice, I mean that there is more than one way in the spiritual life. It is possible to distinguish three paths in particular: the way of good works, the way of devotion, and the way of knowledge. Every authentic tradition contains all three, though a given religion may emphasize one of them more than the others. In Hindu terms, the paths are *karma yoga*, *bhakti yoga*, and *jnana yoga*. Each corresponds to a somewhat different temperament, for there are also three basic human types: the "passional," whose path is "primarily a penitential one," the "sentimental" or "emotional," in

whom "love and hope constitute the dominant and operative element," and the "intellectual" or "fundamentally contemplative" type,
whose way is through discernment toward Truth. You will understand that we are speaking of tendencies, and not water-tight com-
partments. Each of us has a will for working, a soul for loving, and
an intelligence for knowing. In order to be truly effective, the path
which we take must bring all three elements into play at one level or
another.

The path we shall be following here is that of knowledge or *gnosis*.
A few words about this term are undoubtedly needed. I find that
many people are tempted to dismiss or debunk an exposition of *gnosis* solely because of the word's historical associations with the dual-
istic mythologies of heretical gnosticism. It should be obvious, however, that "to claim that all *gnosis* is false because of gnosticism
amounts to saying, by analogy, that all prophets are false because
there are false prophets." Clearly there is nothing wrong with the
word itself, which simply means *knowledge* in Greek. If it has been
misappropriated by proponents of a false spirituality, whether past
or present, we must simply resolve to be attentive to the contexts in
which we find it. No idea is immune to misuse. The path I shall be
describing is gnostic or jnanic. It is equally metaphysical and esoteric. But these descriptive terms are to be understood with strict
reference to the definitions here supplied. "We wish to be held
responsible solely for what we write ourselves."

Of course, quite apart from the distortions introduced by hetero-
dox theological systems, the aim of making knowledge the key to
one's relationship with God is itself going to be a puzzle for some.
When they are told that "*gnosis* is our participation in the 'perspective' of the Divine Subject," or that "esoterism looks to the nature of
things" and "views the Universe not from the human standpoint but
'from the standpoint of God,'" they are likely to object along one of
two lines: either as religious believers of a devotional bent or as
philosophical skeptics.

On the one hand, believers of a bhaktic type are frequently put off
by the claims of *gnosis* on the grounds that knowledge is too cold and
cerebral, that it puffs a man up, and that it is at cross purposes with
the faith and humility which we should have before God. It is under-
standable, temperamentally speaking, that "*bhaktas* have a certain
interest in depreciating the intelligence," and they are doubtless
right to be wary of intellectual pride. But this pride, "or what is

believed to be such," is too often rejected "only to be replaced by an attitude of pride towards the Intellect," a pride woven of resentment and seeking to bring all things down to the lowest and least demanding level. If you stop to think about it, none of us can follow a spiritual way, let alone describe it to others, without using our minds to some extent, and that fact in this case results in considerable irony. What are we to make of the man who knows better than others that knowledge is of no importance?

The alleged incompatibility between mere knowledge and authentic or saving faith is sometimes expressed as an "irreducible opposition between intellection and grace." It is assumed that the wish to understand metaphysical principles or to discover esoteric truths fails to respect the Divine initiative, that it amounts to building a Tower of Babel. Man should instead wait patiently for the inspirations and assistance of God, who will provide all that we need in His own good time. This is to forget, however, that grace means gift, and that the whole of our existence, our minds included, is continuously being given at each moment by Heaven. "Intellection is also a grace, but it is a static and innate grace" unlike certain more obviously miraculous gifts upon which the devotional temperament characteristically bases its relationship with God. Furthermore, "there can be absolutely no reason why this kind of grace should not be a possibility and should never be manifested, seeing that by its very nature it cannot not be." What the theologians call special or supernatural revelation enters into a context already established by general or natural revelation, and this natural revelation is proportioned in turn to an intelligence with the capacity to recognize the revelation for what it is. The way of knowledge takes as its starting point this essential, fundamental capacity.

A second, very different sort of objection will come from the skeptic. Tell him that you have entered upon the way of spiritual knowledge, and he will begin at once to insist that such knowledge is impossible. Unlike the man of faith, he is not concerned to protect the Divine mystery from impiety and compromise. Having himself no fear of impiety, he would instead have you question whether such a mystery exists at all, whether it is anything more than a human invention, and whether—even if there is such a thing—our very limited minds could ever grasp it. Tell him that "human intelligence coincides in its essence with certainty of the Absolute" or that "the principle of knowledge does not of itself imply any limitation" since "to know is to know all that is knowable," and he will think you are mad.

I am sure that you are familiar with this second response, for it is all but pervasive today, especially in certain academic quarters, where the only absolute is the claim that there are no absolutes. Man, we are told, is a relative, finite, conditioned being, whose awareness of the world is restricted to his empirical or physical environment and distorted by his individual or subjective viewpoint. Limitation, fragmentation, and partiality are therefore inevitable, and to admit this is to discard forever all pretensions to objective and metaphysical insight. An adequate exposition of the way of knowledge is obviously going to have to take account of such criticisms if it hopes to go anywhere. I cannot very well ask you to join me on this path without confronting these reservations head on. Even if you are of a type to be attracted by *gnosis*, the very fact that you live at the present moment of history means that to some extent you will have absorbed the skepticism of your environment, and we need to allow for this fact as we proceed.

Truth cannot be properly sought until one has first conclusively resisted the diabolical suggestion that there is no such thing, and I shall try to show how to do that in the pages which follow. If I do not at this point give the same amount of attention to the first objection, to the devotional or religious resistance to knowledge, it is for the simple reason that the *jnani* or gnostic readily agrees with the *bhakta*'s defense of faith, his emphasis on love, and his demand for humility. These are indeed essential to the spiritual life, as is the grace which grants them, and they are not to be neglected by those seeking to know. But the case of the skeptic is altogether different. Love and knowledge are compatible, indeed complementary, but doubt and knowledge are not. The metaphysician must therefore refuse to countenance even the slightest skepticism, for his way "is founded, not upon doubt, but upon analogy and, more profoundly, upon identity both intellectual and existential." We shall be examining this identity later, but before we can do so with any conviction or seriousness, the fallacy of doubt will need to be exposed.

In the meantime, you may simply be wondering about our choice of paths. I have admitted that others are possible. Why knowledge? The answer is contained in the aphorism at the head of this chapter. It may appear trivial, but I assure you that it is filled with meaning. "Knowledge is one and indivisible." This implies at least two things.

It means first that to know anything in fact is to know everything in principle. To know something as simple as 2 + 2 = 4—really to know it, and to know that you know it—is to know that the truth in question is absolute, and that no contingency can stand between you and this certainty. And yet to know that there is nothing between, no boundaries to pass and no gaps to fill in, is to realize that this same truth was within you already. It means seeing that "the mystery of certitude" results from the fact that "the truth is inscribed in the very substance of our spirit" and that "we are what we are able to know." I do not pretend that this point is obvious. If you are thinking that we ought to consider it further, I agree, and an opportunity will be provided shortly.

But allow me for the moment to sketch a second implication of the aphorism. It also means that knowledge is its own proof, its own guarantee or defense. Where good works and devotion are directed to something extrinsic, an object outside themselves, the object of knowledge is intrinsic to that knowledge. "One can love something false without love ceasing to be what it is; but one cannot 'know' falsehood in a similar way." The way of the gnostic or esoterist thus has a certain logical or methodological primacy when compared to the other paths, though I hasten to specify that this is not to make any claims about the capacity or worth of any given man of the intellectual type. The point is just that "knowledge cannot be under illusion as to its object without ceasing to be what it is; error always implies a privation of knowledge, whereas sin does not imply a privation of will."

It follows from all this that in an age such as ours, an age of agnosticism and cynicism at one extreme and spiritual confusion and credulity at the other, the way of knowledge offers certain important benefits which the serious seeker would do well to consider. Can one still approach God solely by obeying and loving Him? Of course. Would it be more appropriate for some people to proceed in those ways than to concern themselves with metaphysics? Yes, it would be. Is their choice second rate? Definitely not. I spell all this out very carefully, for esoterism sometimes appears to the misinformed as an elitist perspective. In fact, however, "the idea that non-esoterists by definition lack intelligence, or that esoterists are *de facto* necessarily possessed of it, does not in any case enter our mind."

And yet it remains true that while certain types of men may not be obliged to avail themselves of *gnosis* in their own particular jour-

neys, knowledge is very much needed for the defense of true spirituality in general, and now more than ever. Knowledge has a double
advantage. It can help us distinguish the Truth from the poisonous
claims of those who say falsely that they have it, and it can protect
that Truth from the withering denunciations of those who say falsely
that no one has it. Only esoterism can "restore the lost truth by referring to the total Truth," and it alone "can satisfy the imperious needs
created by the philosophic and scientific positions of the modern
world."

I hope to help you see why as we proceed.

⊹ Chapter 2 ⊹

Thinking the Unthinkable

Wisdom cannot start from the intention of expressing the ineffable; rather it intends to furnish points of reference which permit us to open ourselves to the ineffable to the extent possible, and according to what is foreseen by the Will of God.

I promised to talk further about the problem of skepticism. But before I do so, we would be wise to pause for a moment to consider the role of reason in metaphysics. Several questions may have occurred to you already. What precisely is the aim of thinking in the spiritual life? How much is to be expected of a discursive exposition like the one I am giving you? How far can human language take us in the direction of God?

Two extremes must be avoided: on the one hand a rationalism which would give too much value to logic; and on the other hand a fideism which would give it too little value, or even no value at all. The way of knowledge lies between.

You must understand, in the first place, that "logic is nothing other than the science of mental coordination, of rational conclusion," and that it therefore "cannot attain to the universal and the transcendent by its own resources." In fact, logic as such, like the reason or discursive mind which employs it, can attain nothing on

17

its own on any level, even that of empirical nature. Reason needs data in order to function. These data may be supplied by physical perception, inspiration, or Revelation, or they may be derived from the conclusions reached through another operation of reason. But reason cannot generate its own raw material. It would be unreasonable and illogical to suppose that it should. It is equally absurd to assume that realities which exceed the limits of our physical senses are therefore beyond the reach of logic, though this is a common mistake. The first lesson of metaphysics is that the rational or logical, on the one hand, and the empirical or physical, on the other, are not the same. "The rationalism of a frog living at the bottom of a well is to deny the existence of mountains: this is logic of a kind, perhaps, but it has nothing to do with reality."

A second point to insist on is that the rules of human thought are not merely subjective conventions. They are instead reflections within us of the cosmos outside, just as this cosmos is a reflection in turn of its Creator. "The principles of noncontradiction and of sufficient reason are rooted in the Divine Intellect," and this means that in drawing valid conclusions from true premises, we are repeating in a way—although inversely—the very creation of the universe. I must ask for your patience. This is not a claim that I expect you to admit at first glance. It will be necessary to return to this axiom. Do notice in the meantime, however, that it is closely bound up with the unity and indivisibility of knowledge. If to know anything in fact is to know everything in principle, then that logic must be considered principial which permits us to recognize in the case of a given fact, however ordinary, that its truth necessarily excludes its falsehood. It is in view of this universal dimension of thought that the metaphysician appeals to our intelligence, for he knows that "no religion has ever imposed on the human mind, or ever could have imposed, an idea which logic was incapable of approaching in any way; religion addresses itself to man, and man is thought."

Nevertheless, though our logic is rooted ultimately in the Logic— that is, the *Logos* or Intellect—of God, one must admit that "there are in God aspects that are independent of all limitative logic," and it is from these that "the cosmic play and the musical aspect of things arise." For this reason, the instinct of the religious believer who is troubled by the pretensions of the rationalist is undoubtedly sound. God is the source of our logical powers. They begin within Him, and by following their lead, we may trace them back to a knowledge of their Source. And yet precisely to the extent that they do begin in Him, He is more than they are, and it would therefore be illogical to expect them to be more than pointers. The same thing could be said about our thinking on every level. Even a physical object exceeds our attempts at exhaustive comprehension or description. All the more is this going to be so when we turn our minds to the "Divine Essence," which "eludes logic" precisely because, unlike the Divine *Logos* or Intellect, "it is strictly undefinable"—undefinable, if you will, by definition. In making this distinction between a Divine Essence and a Divine Intellect, I am getting rather ahead of our story, however. When we come back to this distinction later, please remember that it is closely related to the present question about the limits of thought. God is indeed beyond our thinking, and therefore beyond our logic. But it is only insofar as we can think about Him with the logic He lends us that we can see this is so. If rational thought cannot exhibit God fully, it is for the same reason that we cannot see seeing or hear hearing. God is essentially undefinable because He is too close, not because He is too far away.

We shall certainly have to use our heads in what follows, for this is the way of knowledge. But our thinking will be invited, even forced at times, to discern its own boundaries with a view to opening up and out of itself. The Truth would indeed be forever beyond our grasp, just as the skeptics suppose, were it not for the fact that "sufficiently adequate thought, however tentative, can actualize a sudden awareness pertaining to a completely different dimension from the chain of mental operations." It is for the sake of this change of dimensions that *gnosis* is taught. "Pure metaphysics is essentially symbolist and descriptive, not literal and conjectural," for its masters know that "a doctrinal formulation is perfect, not because it exhausts the whole of infinite Truth on the level of mental logic, for that it cannot do, but because it realizes a mental form which is capable of communicating a ray of that Truth to one who is fit to receive it." I have said that we shall be turning to some proofs very shortly. But I must warn you that "'proof,' on the level in question, is a key or a symbol, a means of drawing back a veil rather than of providing actual illumination." Strictly speaking, esoterism "'indicates' rather than proves," and its dialectic takes the form of "a guideline or an *aide-memoire*, since it is impossible to prove the Absolute outside itself."

Allow me to close with two analogies. Wood is not fire any more than logic is intuitive insight. But if you rub two pieces of wood together with sufficient intensity, heat is produced, and suddenly a flame springs forth. So it is with our thoughts. We cannot exactly rub them together, but we can bring them into contact in a mode befitting their kind of reality, and we can press them against each other by applying the pressure of logical consistency. Handle them loosely—let them mean just anything, show no concern for sequence, coherence, or proportion—and they will remain mere mental notions. But handle them with discipline and rigor, and they can become with God's help supports for the combustion of spiritual knowledge.

The way of *gnosis* can also be compared to aerating soil. As we proceed, we are going to be making numerous distinctions between various aspects and angles of vision. At no point will the canons of logic be violated: no A will be considered as not-A at the same time and in the same respect. And yet it will be necessary to examine certain A's from alternative points of view and thus in different respects, and hence to accept "positions which are seemingly opposed, but which in reality are situated on the same circumference, invisible at first." We encountered the most important of these polarities already, in the Introduction, in the observation that God is both outside and inside the world.

You will be asked to admit, in short, that "there are questions to which the answer is at once 'yes' and 'no,'" and to cultivate a certain "interior mobility" or conceptual plasticity. This procedure will prove very frustrating as long as you harbor any secret wish "to enclose universal Reality in an exclusive and exhaustive 'explanation.'" My advice is to get accustomed instead to looking along the formulations you are asked to consider, rather than directly at them. Try to think of the distinctions we make as so many furrows in your mind, which thus like the soil of a newly plowed field may be opened to the nourishing air of God's presence. And remember that "the most explicit metaphysical doctrine will always take it as axiomatic that every doctrine is only error when confronted with the Divine Reality in itself; but a provisional, indispensable, and salutary 'error,' which contains and communicates the virtuality of Truth."

Chapter 3

Proofs of God

Metaphysics cannot be taught to everyone, but if it could be there would be no atheists.

T he seeker who goes looking for spiritual answers today is usually searching for more than just detail. Of course he would
like to know what God is like and what God asks of him. He may
even be curious as to how the world came about or, perhaps more
importantly, how it will end. But before all of that, before he can
begin to digest the specifics, the inquirer needs some initial reassur-
ance that there is such a thing as a God in the first place. He wants
to be certain that God exists. Some men have always aspired to this
certainty, wishing to verify beyond all shadow of doubt what they do
not see, and yet believe. But an aspiration which in times past was
more or less confined to the few has in our day become of increasing
importance to everyone who is serious about the religious life. Wide-
spread skepticism, agnosticism, and atheism have made all of us
realize, on one level or another, that accepting a doctrine on authority is only the beginning of the spiritual journey.

As I pointed out earlier, an adequate response to the question you
have asked will therefore need to be large enough to embrace both
a defense of the very legitimacy of the spiritual life, at one end of the
spectrum, and practical advice on realizing the full fruits of that life,

at the other. In Christian theological terms, you need apologetics, which is the defense of doctrine; dogmatics, or the exposition of doctrine; ethics, or the application of doctrine; and an ascetical or mystical theology leading to the verification of doctrine. In this chapter, I would like to focus briefly on defense—on what we might call esoteric apologetics. Do not be misled by this term, however. As the last chapter was designed to make clear, it would be a mistake to go looking for discursive arguments from a metaphysician or to expect to find logical formulas for dealing with the skeptics, whether within or around you. Our path will be one of indication and pointing. I shall ask you to look esoterically—to look within what you see and, more importantly, within your seeing.

I noted at the start of this chapter that "metaphysics cannot be taught to everyone." It is important, however, not to give the wrong impression or to provoke again the charge of elitism. I spent some time earlier trying to counter this charge, and I certainly do not want to discourage you now by implying that only scholars should be pursuing this path. If metaphysics cannot be taught to everyone, it is often less a question of intellectual ability or capacity than of a willingness to learn. Undoubtedly, as with any teaching on any subject, a certain intelligence is presupposed. And yet the most important thing in this case—the only indispensable qualification—is childlike wonder and contemplativity, not mere mental quickness or a memory for facts. "In the spiritual order a proof is of assistance only to the man who wishes to understand and who, by virtue of this wish, has already in some measure understood." On the other hand, such a proof "is of no practical use to one who, deep in his heart, does not want to change his position, and whose philosophy merely expresses this desire." The fact that you are sincerely seeking to know the Truth, while no guarantee that your mind has the power to come to terms with it rationally, is an excellent sign that your heart will be able to discern what it needs. Be assured in any case that "there are demonstrations which, whether they are understood or not, are sufficient in themselves and indeed constitute pillars of metaphysical doctrine."

These demonstrations or proofs are of two kinds. One is related to the world and the other to ourselves, one to the object known and the other to the knowing subject. The former kind is suggestive, while the latter is decisive.

The objects of the world around us "'prove,' or rather 'manifest,' Divine Reality" in several ways. They do so first of all through their very existence. After all, "to exist is no small matter," and "the proof is that no man can extract from nothingness a single speck of dust." It is only our familiarity with things which could have dulled us to the utterly stupendous fact that something is not nothing, whatever that something might be and however seemingly trivial. To look afresh upon the miracle of existence is to see that "the hiatus between nothingness and the least of objects is absolute, and in the last analysis this absoluteness is that of God."

Where existence as such manifests the absoluteness of God, the diversity, multiplicity, and extension of things through space and time are signs of the infinitude or plenitude of God. Just as nothing comes from nothing, which is why there must be the Absolute, so the more cannot come from the less, which is why there must be the Infinite. The very fecundity and variety of creatures cannot be accounted for by reducing them to their parts or contents. They are to be explained only by reference to an unlimited Principle which contains them eternally. Space, time, form, number, substance, and the other "universal categories" or conditions of existence, together with the limitless "modes of expanse or extension" by which things are deployed within these conditions, are so many open doors onto the infinitude, and hence the immanence, of the Divine.

If existence points to the Absolute and diversity to the Infinite, the specific qualities, capacities, and faculties of creatures point us toward Perfection or the Good. I shall be developing this insight later when we discuss the role of Beauty in the spiritual life. As we shall see, such things as colors, shapes, textures, and tones, both in themselves individually and in their differentiation and hierarchical arrangements, would not be able to convey the meaning they do were there no Meaning or Goodness from which they might borrow. In connection with this same point, mention should be made as well of "privative phenomena"—that is, things which are defective, ugly, disproportionate, or even maleficent in one way or another. Such things are proofs, paradoxically and *a contrario*, of the same Perfection, since "the absence of a good proves, or indicates, the possibility of the presence of that good." Our recognition that a thing is bad implies our cognition of what is good, and at the same time it can reinforce and even deepen that knowledge.

The fact and features of the world will be more than enough proof of God for the contemplative man who is sensitive to the qualitative aspect of things. The skeptic will demand something stronger and more decisive, however. This can be found in a second kind of demonstration, which is based upon the knowing subject. I said that we would need to look, but also that we should look at our looking. If we wish to know God with complete certitude, we must bend our thinking back on itself, for only then can we find "the things that have never been unknown," but which for that reason "seem to be at the same time those that men have the greatest difficulty in learning."

Ask yourself the question, "Why is it that 'I' am 'I'?" And "why is the 'other' an other?" Have you ever stopped to consider that the first person singular personal pronoun is the only word which we all apply to completely different things, but which always means the same thing? How is it that we can still communicate? If I used the word X to name a tree, and you used it to label an elephant, and someone else to signify the sun, and so on and on, with no one ever intending a univocal object, we would all be completely confused. But not in this case. Although few people make it a topic of deliberate reflection, each of us intuitively knows that *I* means more than *me*, that there is a fundamental difference between the one who says *I* and the individual thus named. This difference, deeply pondered— "the phenomenon of an 'I' that is unique, yet multiple"—can lead the person who is "sensitive to the essence of things" to "the dazzling intuition of the absolute Subject, whose unicity, at once transcendent and immanent, is unambiguous." It can lead, in other words, to God.

I can make the same point by inviting you to notice that the subject of any given act of knowing can never be captured as an object of knowledge. Try as I will, I can never slip up on the *I* unawares or catch it dozing. I cannot exhibit it, confront it, or categorize it. It is always eluding my grasp precisely because it is the one who is grasping. It is always disappearing before my vision, because it is that vision. Just when I think I might see it, it turns out to be the light of that seeing itself. But what do we call something which is by its very nature insusceptible to exhibition and description, something upon which everything we know depends, but which is itself dependent on nothing? If we are metaphysicians, we call it absolute. And we insist for this reason that "an intelligence that refuses to admit the Absolute does not take account of the total Reality to which it is proportioned." Can you see why the "intelligence when not atrophied—the pure, intuitive, contemplative Intellect—allows no doubt on this subject, the 'proofs' being in its very substance"?

If not, it is probably because you have been around certain philosophers too much, and you are undoubtedly ready to pounce with objections. You will say that I have proven nothing. The grammatical point about the uniqueness of a certain pronoun is merely a verbal trick. As for the elusive character of the knowing subject, this is admittedly a curious phenomenon, but curiosity is not itself proof. The fact that my consciousness is not a distinct object of consciousness tells us nothing either way about God. In fact, all that we really know about our subjectivity is that it is anything but absolute. We know that man is conditioned by his situation in history—that what he can know comes to him through his empirical senses alone and is then colored, shaped, and thus distorted by his unique psychology.

But please take careful note of something very important. Those who would have you raise such objections are talking about *me* and not *I*. In seeming to agree that consciousness is no object of consciousness, they miss the point totally, for the agreement is only apparent. In fact they are thinking all the while of consciousness in the past tense, and they end up treating it precisely as an object. The metaphysician calls their attention to the one who knows now, but they have inattentively inserted the remembered residue of the one who knew, to which they attribute all the limitations and distortions in question. Meanwhile they remain smugly unaware that the alleged truth of their epistemological criticisms involves them in a self-contradiction. For the constraints which they would place upon human knowledge are clearly not meant at that moment to apply to themselves, the present knowers, who are therefore free to pontificate on what is possible for the rest of mankind.

I hope you can see why the claim "that man can never pass beyond human subjectivity is the most gratuitous and contradictory of hypotheses." If no one can transcend the conditions of his environment or go beyond the attitudes, biases, preconceptions, moods, and other refracting elements of his individual soul, "who then defines this 'subjectivity' as such?" One of two things: either the skeptic is simply not listening when he is told that "without the Absolute, the capacity to conceive it would have no cause," or else he is unable or unwilling to exert the effort it takes to remark the difference between this capacity, on the one hand, and the resulting conception, on the other. The esoterist is not talking about an idea or notion of the Absolute which we may happen to have entertained. He is pointing us to the power or scope of intelligence itself, which proves in its operation that there must be a God. But this will be understood only by the man who is prepared to reflect upon the very act of his knowing: not some vague philosophical generality, but this act—his act—right now. I trust you are beginning to see why doctrine must go hand in hand with method. Metaphysical comprehension is to no purpose without spiritual discipline. The proper use of the intelligence in this domain requires a will to concentrate.

We simply must keep attention pinned on itself, and not on some topic or idea or argument, even the argument that one happens to be making at this very moment. The esoteric apologist must be rather like a wrestler, constantly adjusting his grip as attention shifts and wanders. And he must be prepared for the fact that "in our days, there is no fear of the contradiction inherent in questioning the subject, the knower, in its intrinsic and irreplaceable aspect; intelligence as such is called in question, it is even 'examined,' without wondering 'who' examines it." In harping as he does on the relativity and contingency of all human knowledge, the skeptic is constantly forgetting, or neglecting, the living subject of the present instant, substituting instead his memory of who he was just a second ago, and this memory, of course, is not intrinsic or irreplaceable. It is not the knower himself, but just what the skeptic or relativist says: a conditioned bit of finitude. Inattentive to the one who knows now, he therefore only smiles when we tell him that man's "extraordinarily profound and comprehensive subjectivity can be explained only by an absolute which substantially prefigures it and projects it into accidence"—that is, only by God. He is convinced we must be joking.

Oddly enough, the incomprehension, inattention, and self-contradiction that I have been describing are like a further and final proof of the "theophanic phenomenon of consciousness"—a proof, in other words, that God appears through our knowing. Supposing you tell someone that if A = B and B = C, then A = C, and he says, I cannot see why; I want you to prove it. Does not his incomprehension make clear the fundamentally intuitive nature of the proof he demands? Is it not a demonstration *a contrario* of what makes for real certitude? Think about it. "If the optic nerve has to be examined in order to be sure that vision is real, it will likewise be necessary to examine that which examines the optic nerve, an absurdity which proves in its own indirect way that knowledge of suprasensible things is intuitive and cannot be other than intuitive." We shall be turning next to a closer consideration of this intuition.

✤ Chapter 4 ✤

The Intellect

It is indispensable to know at the outset that there are truths inherent in the human spirit that are as if buried in the "depths of the heart," which means that they are contained as potentialities or virtualities in the pure Intellect.

Our topic last time was proofs. We could summarize our discussion by saying that God's existence is proved whenever one sees "the Infinite in space and time, the Absolute or necessary Being in the existence of things, Perfection or the Good in qualities and faculties, and the supreme Self in the prodigy of the perceiving subjectivity." Let me remind you that when the spiritual teacher offers us a proof, he assumes that we are seriously seeking the Truth, and he expects us to realize that his words are but pointers. Truth cannot be packaged and served up for the asking. We shall have to do some work for ourselves.

Specifically, we must begin to activate our intuitive power. We have been asked to see—to see the Infinite, to see the Absolute, to see the Good, and to see the Self—and not merely to think about them rationally. The seeing which we are to exercise is certainly not an empirical or physical perception alone. What, then, is it?

Following as always the lead of the perennial philosophers, I shall refer to this mode of vision as the Intellect. The Intellect is the fac-

27

ulty or power of immediate discernment, unobstructed by the boundaries of physical objects and unaffected by the limitations of historical circumstance. It is the power of seeing things as they are, "in their total context," and therefore both in their "relativity" and in their "metaphysical transparency." In short, the Intellect is what enables us to be objective and to take account solely of the nature of things, without the intervention of private interest or special pleading. Intellect is the name for the power, and intellection is its act.

It is necessary to guard this definition very carefully. Intellect is one of those words whose meanings have been cheapened over time. In most contexts, it is now treated as a synonym for reason or mind. We talk about certain people as intellectuals when all we really mean is that they have a disposition toward speculation or other modes of discursive thinking. An extra effort will therefore be needed to keep the specified sense in focus and to avoid confusing it with apparent equivalents.

The Intellect is in fact very different from the discursive mind or reason. "The mind is analogous to the Intellect insofar as it is a kind of intelligence, but is opposed to it by its limited, indirect, and discursive character." While reason operates one step at a time, proceeding by stages from premises to conclusions, the Intellect goes straight to the conclusion, although in this case to speak of a conclusion could be a little misleading, for there is no summing up or synthesis of prior particularities. "Reason obtains knowledge like a man walking about and exploring a countryside by successive discoveries, whereas the Intellect contemplates the same countryside from a mountain height." Reason conceives—that is, it holds things together. But the Intellect perceives. It cuts right through those things, directly apprehending their esoteric meaning or essence. It is to the spiritual or suprasensible order what vision and the other physical senses are to the material or empirical order. And this is why the content of the Intellect can be approached by the reason only through analogies. It is no more possible to show the reason what the Intellect sees than to prove the existence of color to a blind man. "To ask for a proof of intellection is like asking for the proof of the adequacy of our elementary sensations."

Furthermore, unlike rational thought, the Intellect is not dependent on information coming from the outside. "Direct and supramental intellection is in reality a 'remembering' and not an 'acquisition,'" and this "'remembering' is nothing other than an actualization, thanks to an occasional external cause, or to an internal inspiration, of an eternal potentiality of the intellective substance." Intellectual intuition is the result of an explication or unfolding of the substance of the Intellect itself. "In properly intellectual or heart knowledge, the principial realities grasped by the heart are themselves prolonged in intellection."

This last observation helps to point us toward two further characteristics of the intuitive faculty. To say that it resides in the heart is to say, first, that it has a concrete, existential dimension, unlike the reason which resides in the brain and is strictly mental or cerebral. Seated in the heart, which is the center of man, the Intellect contains and prolongs all our faculties, including not only intelligence as such, but the will and the sentiment or feeling soul. In fact, the body too is a prolongation of the Intellect, which is refracted or polarized within the individual man into both corporal and psychic aspects. "Mind and body both reflect the Intellect, or rather mind and body 'are' the Intellect, by bipolarized reflection in the flux of peripheral Existence." When we discuss the degrees of Reality in the next meditation, I shall be explaining where precisely Existence fits into the ontological hierarchy or chain of Being, and we shall begin to see that this polarization or complementary opposition is rooted in the Supreme Reality itself. For the moment, the point is simply to make sure you realize that the Intellect is no abstraction, but a real power having palpable consequences.

Perhaps another way to express this teaching is to say that the Intellect is the presence in man of what in a plant causes it "irresistibly to turn towards the light." Indeed, the Intellect is operative throughout nature and is manifest, not only in the vegetable order, but—to take just two examples—in the magnetic properties of the lodestone and in the migratory instinct of birds. It is the principle of order and design which one may discern in everything from a crystal to a hive of bees. In man, unlike the rest of the terrestrial creation, this principle can become aware of itself, whether in the intelligence as intuition, in the will as conscience, or in the soul as a sense of the sacred. But though conscious in man, or at least potentially so, it is no less immediate, concrete, and existential than it is in the mineral, the plant, or the animal.

It was said that the "principial realities" are themselves "prolonged in intellection," and this leads me to make a second, somewhat more difficult point. Intellection is an explication, not an acquisition, because the Intellect is already what it knows. It "coincides, in its innermost nature, with the very Being of things." This is why intellectual intuition is not subject to the conditions imposed upon reason, those conditions which the skeptic so delights in exposing. Reason by its very nature must aspire to a truth outside itself. But the Intellect is its own outside. It has nowhere to go, no intervening gaps between itself and its object, for "in the Intellect, the subject is the object, 'being,' and the object is the subject, 'knowing': whence comes absolute certitude." The Intellect is in back of the very distinction between subject and object, inside and outside, mind and body. They are contained in it, so that it cannot be made to fit entirely within either one of them, though where one finds it initially is on the subjective side of that polarity, in the depths of one's knowing, whence it opens out into every possible object of consciousness, since "all possible knowledge is inscribed in its very substance."

I began by calling the Intellect a faculty, but it is not a faculty which you or I possess, or which is at our disposal in quite the same way as our hands and feet. If anything, it possesses us, for the Intellect is a "universal faculty" existing on a level that surpasses a given man's individuality. Its certitudes are contained "not in the thinking ego, but in the transpersonal substance of the human intelligence." It follows that no one can take credit for the knowledge granted him through the Intellect. When I said earlier that we need to activate our intuitive power, this was a bit imprecise. We must indeed act, for the spiritual life includes effort, but essentially this effort means getting ourselves out of the way, creating a space so that God can act in us. Though a man may be the beneficiary of the Intellect, he is by no means its author. Its author is God, in whose knowledge man may participate through what we have called the "static and innate grace" of intellection, but in the face of whose absoluteness man remains always a creature and servant.

We could say, in fact, that "the Intellect is in subjective mode what Revelation is in objective mode." Or in geometrical terms, "the Intellect is a ray rather than a circle; it 'emanates' from God rather than 'reflecting' Him," reflection being what we find in the reason or mind. This is why the metaphysician often describes the Intellect as being "uncreated and uncreatable." Coming from God, it is not just a creature. But neither is it God Himself. It is at once more than man and less than God. And yet it is not so much a third thing between them as it is "the permanent manifestation of the Divine in the human microcosm."

I realize that this is at first sight a most perplexing idea. We need to go slowly and give ourselves time to get used to these unusual propositions. How it is that something might be of God but not God—how a reality can be neither this nor that, nor both, nor neither—is the subject of our next two discussions. In the meantime, perhaps you are at least beginning to glimpse why we "say that there is an Absolute Reality, not because we believe it, but because we know it, and we know it because we are it in our transpersonal Intellect."

❧ Chapter 5 ❧

Degrees of Reality

In metaphysics, as in every other realm, it is necessary to know how to put everything in its place.

*T*o be or not to be is actually not the question.

In starting in this deliberately paradoxical way, I mean to be playful, to tease your thinking. But I am perfectly serious, too. And I am hoping if possible to provoke a level of engagement which reflects this blend of earnestness and play. Reality itself displays such a combination, and we must become in a manner like the Real if we mean to know it. Woven from exceptions that prove the rule, the universe is a tapestry of both necessities and possibilities—of identities, analogies, and oppositions—where momentary position means instant displacement. And yet there is no lawlessness here. If Reality must be danced or sung, no formula or science being fully adequate to it, there is nevertheless an established choreography and a definite rhythm to the song. In order to grasp metaphysical doctrine, we must become accustomed to a kaleidoscope of shifting perspectives—with the understanding, however, that "these perspectives result from objective reality and not from human arbitrariness."

To be or not to be is not the question because Reality is a matter of degrees. This idea is essential to our comprehension of the Truth, and it is constantly stressed by the perennial philosophy. It is at the same time an idea very foreign to the thinking of most people today. Consider the distinctions you ordinarily make. The things around us are compared with each other quantitatively, of course. This one is bigger than that one. This one is heavier, while that one is faster. Systems and instruments of measurement exist to confirm these differences. When it comes to quality, however, especially in the aesthetic realm, our comparisons are usually subjective. I like this poem better than that one, we say, or this painting seems to me more attractive. This subjectivism or relativism has come more and more to encroach upon the moral domain, with the result that the very goodness or justice of actions is said by some to be a matter of personal preference.

But my concern at the moment is not with relativism. What I would like you to notice is that even among those people who may admit the existence of a universal moral standard or objective Beauty, it is the very rare person who identifies this standard or this Beauty with Being itself, except perhaps in a strictly theoretical way. I mean more than theory, however. I am talking about an effective or practical identification. For most of us, practically speaking, either a thing exists or it does not, and if it does exist, its degree of Being—supposing we ever used such a phrase—is associated with some measurement of its quantity, like the degrees on a thermometer or a protractor.

I must ask you to begin looking at the world very differently. The formulations we are about to examine are not going to make any practical difference to your spiritual life until they are coupled with a certain change of perspective, a fundamental alteration of vision. Your study of the doctrine of degrees in the Real must go hand in hand with a genuine effort to see why a good man, for example, is more real than a bad man. The man who is good may well be shorter, of course, or in some other quantitative way less imposing than the man who is not. Nevertheless his virtue betokens an amplitude and a solidity which are proof against vicissitude and change, marking him as one who is more integrally real than the man who is vicious. We may say, in a similar way, that there is a greater degree of Being in the beautiful than in the ugly, and that a cause is more real than its effect. Can you begin to see why?

Let me draw two pictures. Picture, on the one hand, a vertical line which is intersected at right angles by a series of horizontal parallels. The vertical axis is an image of Reality. The line is single and continuous because Reality is one. The horizontal lines are demarcations of various levels within the Real. These lines are multiple because the Real is a plenitude of possibilities embracing genuine differences. Picture, on the other hand, a central point surrounded by a series of concentric circles or spheres connected to each other by lines emerging from the center. In this case, the circles or spheres are the levels of Reality, the radii represent its continuity, and the center permits us to visualize the singularity or uniqueness of the Real. Whatever the picture, we must get used to the idea that depending upon the respect in which we envision it, Reality is at once unicity, totality, and unity.

At this point, I must introduce some technical terms, and the pictures should help to make remembering them easier. So far in our discussions, I have confined myself to using familiar words in referring to the various aspects or levels of Reality. I have spoken, for example, about God and about the cosmos or universe without attempting to provide any definitions or to distinguish them in any special way. But it is time to begin being more precise. The seasoned traveler knows the importance of having a good map, one that indicates even subtle changes in his intended path, especially if the terrain is difficult. In undertaking the spiritual journey, our concern is no different. It is necessary to take note of the even more subtle differences in the landscape of Reality, and this means dividing the Real into parts—never forgetting, of course, that the Real in itself is still one.

We have a choice. We can start with either the most real or the least real. The former would be found at the top of our vertical axis and the latter at the bottom, along the lowest of the horizontal bars. Or we could use the second image. In this case, the greatest Reality could be placed at the very center in order to accentuate the fact that it is of all things the most inward, hidden within their esoteric heart. At the other extreme, it could be visualized as the space surrounding the outermost sphere, enveloping everything else. In assigning names, I shall begin with what is most real, and I suggest that we keep in mind both diagrams, seeing this Supreme Reality as both the highest and the most inward of things. In this way we can underscore the fact that it is both transcendent and immanent, while at the same time insisting as an essential corollary that "the Transcendent comprises a dimension of immanence, just as for its part the Immanent comprises a dimension of transcendence."

Whether looking to the zenith or the center, we take note first of the Absolute or "necessary Being," which "suffices unto itself" and which "cannot not be." This is the Supreme Reality, in comparison with which everything else is contingent and relative, and we must learn not to confuse this Reality with anything else. "The indispensable doctrinal knowledge is the distinguishing of the Absolute from the contingent." In the terminology of Hindu *Advaita Vedanta*, which the perennial philosophers consider "the most direct possible expression of *gnosis*," this is the distinction between *Atma* and *Maya*. While the idea of the Absolute tends to connote transcendence or height along the vertical axis, the word *Atma*, referring to the Self or absolute Subject—the Supreme Knower at the root of all knowledge—is best represented by the point at the center of the circles. It reminds us that the Source of all things can be thought of as lying deep within us. *Maya* means most simply illusion, and for our purposes it can be equated with relativity. "All other distinctions and valuations derive from this fundamental distinction"—the distinction between the Absolute and the relative.

Now the Absolute is equally the Infinite. Being Absolute, it is necessarily independent of all. But what is universally independent is without any limits. That which cannot not be cannot be restricted. It must therefore be infinite. This point is crucial, for were the Absolute not at the same time the Infinite, the distinction between *Atma* and *Maya* would be a great divide. And were there such a divide, there would be in fact no *Maya* at all. Everything relative would never have been. As it is, however, the infinitude of the Supreme Reality results inevitably in an irresistible radiation by which it lends degrees of its Being to all things, whether in a descending or a centrifugal order.

I have been using the words *Being* and *Reality* more or less interchangeably. I shall continue to do so when it is a question of emphasizing the objective pole of things as distinct from the subjective pole of consciousness. But for the moment, I must insert an amendment. The Supreme Reality, owing precisely to its infinitude, is in this context more accurately understood as Non-Being or Beyond-Being, since it is beyond all restriction or determination. Similarly, as the centermost point with regard to immanence, it may be called "the supra-ontological Subject." What is ontological is a matter of being, but like the transcendent Absolute, the immanent Knower exceeds our very conception of is-ness insofar as that conception has been derived from relative things.

Used in a technical metaphysical way, Being refers to a degree of Reality one step down from the pure Absolute or the Absolute as such. In our second image, it corresponds to the circle closest to the center. Being is the first fruit, as it were, of the Infinite, and it is the highest level of *Maya*. "Beyond-Being—or Non-Being—is Reality absolutely unconditioned, while Being is Reality insofar as it determines itself in the direction of its manifestation." It is important to emphasize that while the level of Being is conditioned or relative with respect to the Infinite, it is nevertheless far beyond the relativities with which we are familiar in the world around us. It participates in the eternity and impassibility of the supremely Real. As a metacosmic Reality beyond all Manifestation, it is sometimes called the uncreated *Logos*. From the point of view of *Atma*, Being is relative, but from the point of view of creation, it is absolute. And this is why it can be referred to, paradoxically, as the relative Absolute. "There cannot be an 'absolutely relative,' but there is a 'relative absolute.'"

Being corresponds to the personal God of the various religious traditions, who is the Creator, Legislator, Preserver, and Judge of the world. Religious believers are sometimes scandalized by this teaching, for they mistakenly think that it demotes or belittles God. But this is false. Far from making God less, it can assist us in seeing that the Divine Person opens onto a Reality far more stupendous than we ever imagined. For the distinction between Beyond-Being and Being is a distinction in fact *in divinis*—that is, within God Himself—and it is intended to point us ultimately toward a more adequate valuation of His plenitude. To be sure, this "key notion of *Maya in divinis*," of relativity in God, is not an idea that you will find outside a purely metaphysical exposition, and it may take some getting used to. The same distinction was noted earlier, in our reflections on the limits of logic, in the difference between the Divine Essence and the Divine Intellect or uncreated *Logos*. It will be stressed several times in what follows, though unless otherwise stated, when speaking of God, I shall continue to mean both Essence and Person. "The word 'God' does not and cannot admit of any restriction for the simple reason that God is 'all that is purely principial.'"

Taken together, Beyond-Being and Being constitute what the metaphysician calls the Divine Principle, and here a second fundamental discernment must be noted, between Principle and Manifestation. To return again to our diagrams, this new distinction of degrees can be pictured along the vertical axis as a line of demarcation within the domain of *Maya* and below the previous boundary between the Absolute and the relative. Or you could think of it as a second circle proceeding out from the Supreme Center. Manifestation is also referred to as Existence or Creation. "Just as Being is the Word or Name of Beyond-Being, so too the world—or Existence—is the Utterance of Being, of the personal God." Calling it Existence or Creation emphasizes the discontinuity between this degree of Reality and the one which is immediately superior to it, the degree of the relative Absolute, and this is in keeping with God's transcendence. No creature may be considered His equal. On the other hand, calling it Manifestation reminds us of the infinitude of the Supreme Reality, and hence of its immanence. Since nothing is able to enclose or to limit this Reality, it cannot but be everywhere. Whatever exists is an expression of the Real in some way and on some level. All appearances are appearances of it. We shall want to look more carefully into this relationship between what is and what seems in our next meditation.

Finally, within the domain of Creation or Manifestation, a third distinction needs to be made, this time between Heaven and Earth—the celestial and the terrestrial worlds. Here we must draw a horizontal line within the area of our first diagram marked out as Existence. Above this line are the spiritual or angelic worlds of created but formless or supraformal realities, including not only the angels but the transpersonal Intellect or created *Logos*. Below the line is the world of individual or formal Manifestation, which includes both the subtle realm of the soul and the corporal realm of the human body and other physical or material entities. With this last, material level of Manifestation, we come to the lowest and most contingent degree of reality in our universe—to the outermost sphere, furthest of all from the center, which is like the carapace or shell of the invisible worlds.

To sum up: "We may thus distinguish in the total Universe four degrees: Beyond-Being, God-Being, Heaven, and Earth. Beyond-Being and Being taken together—if one may so express it—constitute the Divine Principle; while Heaven and Earth constitute universal Manifestation."

It is time to bring this discussion to a close. I have given you a great deal to ponder, and a pause is advisable before going on. I would simply repeat my opening point about the playfulness of things. Please do not suppose that Reality is going to stand for our dividing it up into such neat little pieces. The various lines we have drawn must not be permitted to obscure the fact that "things are in God and God is in things with a kind of discontinuous continuity." Nor could it be otherwise. In its absoluteness and transcendence, the Supreme Reality cannot but surpass everything else. It would not be going too far to say, in fact, that this Reality is the only Reality: nothing exists except the metaphysical Absolute, which is Unicity. On the other hand, in its infinitude and immanence, the Supreme Reality cannot but be present within everything else, making all things shimmer with its glory. All of Reality is only it: everything which exists is the metaphysical Infinite, which is Totality. And since there is but one Reality, Unicity and Totality must be understood as together constituting an indivisible Unity. The vertical axis intersects every horizontal line, the radii join the center with every circumference, and there is as a consequence a continuous interchange of apparent antinomies, which resolve themselves always into complementary opposites. I shall try to spell out the reason for this interchange in our next meditation.

In the meantime, just a word of encouragement. Please remember that all these terms are but windows, openings or passages leading out of ourselves and into the nature of things. "Metaphysical knowledge" as such "must always be kept essentially distinct from its formulation; and formulation, whatever form it may assume, can never be taken as anything but a symbol of that which in itself is incommunicable." The perennial philosopher will be the first to admit that Reality is much more than even the truest philosophy.

We would not need all these windows if we would just go outside.

Chapter 6

The Doctrine of Illusion

*If there are men apparently of limited intelligence who are
saints and men who are apparently saints who are really of
limited intelligence, and if there are fish that fly and birds
that swim—if God loves in His creation this interplay of
compensations and surprises, this game of hide and seek in
which anything can be anything—this is by virtue of His
infinity which cannot stop at any limits.*

*W*e know that there is a Supreme Reality because it cannot not
be. By its very nature, it is the Absolute. This Absolute,
moreover, is necessarily Infinite, which means that it is utterly
unbounded, free from every restriction or definition, even that of
Being itself. The Infinite gives rise in turn to *Maya* or the relative
since that which is unrestricted by anything, even itself, cannot but
spill over itself. It cannot but radiate, just as the sun cannot but
shine. As the Absolute implies the Infinite, so the Infinite implies
Manifestation.

But this is not the whole story. Though the metaphysician would
have us put everything in its place, he will not let us leave it there.
He will make sure that we understand that these places are constantly shifting position, according to perspective. It is therefore
time to develop our preceding meditation by taking note of two addi-

41

tional points, two further implications of the infinity or plenitude of God. These should be of help to you in coming to terms with what is meant when we say that "the cosmic play of possibilities, which are innumerable, tends towards 'the exception which proves the rule.'"

Since the Real is a unity, there can be degrees but no gaps within it. There can be only one Reality, and as one it is continuous. This is the metaphysical root of the cosmological maxim that nature abhors a vacuum. But now comes the first of my additions. Reality, we have said, is also a unicity—a single, indivisible Essence—and this being so, the idea of degrees or levels must give way to overlappings and encroachments. There cannot be simply this and that. Allowance must be made for this to be in that, and for that to be in this. I am being very abstract, I realize, but I want to give you some sense of the underlying reason for this aspect of the doctrine.

Let us come to specifics. The perennial philosophy teaches that insofar as the Infinite implies Manifestation, Manifestation may be said to be prefigured within it, and this prefiguration is Being or the relative Absolute. Thus there is not only Manifestation below the Principle, but Manifestation in the Principle. It follows that every below is within the above. "The fact that the world is in no way the Divine Substance as such by no means prevents the cosmic substance from being in its own way a modality of the metacosmic Substance." The world is not God, but it may be described as existing within Him. On the other hand, insofar as Manifestation is the expression of the Infinite, the Infinite may be said to be projected within it, and this projection appears in the first place as Heaven or the celestial worlds. There is not only the Principle above Manifestation, but the Principle in Manifestation. Every above is within the below, not just in Heaven but on Earth as well, and it is this which makes possible Revelation, incarnation, intellection, inspiration, and a host of other Divine disclosures. "In and through Being, God 'becomes the world a little' so that in and through Heaven, the world may 'become God a little.' If this be possible, it is by virtue of the metaphysical identity between Principle and Manifestation, an identity which is certainly difficult to express, but witnessed to by all esoterisms."

The essential thing to be grasped is that in being infinite, God is without any edges. The relationship between what is God and what is not God is therefore necessarily fluid, and this is something which no scheme can capture, even one which allows for degrees of Reality.

Whether constituted by axes or circles, diagrams can take us only so far, for "the 'line of demarcation' between God and the world can be thought of in different ways, according to whether one is distinguishing between the ontological Principle and its creation, or between universal Intellect and things, or again between the Absolute and the relative, the Real and the unreal, the Self and its objectivations." If a man would know the Truth, he must be prepared to look along a variety of formulations in which the places of the Real have been differently positioned. It remains true, of course, since God is absolute, that there is "no common measure between the supreme Principle and its cosmic Manifestation, for the latter is nothing of itself, whereas the Principle is only of itself." The true gnostic is most certainly not a pantheist. Nevertheless, since "on our level of reality we do exist, there have to be possible points of contact between us and God; therefore the incommensurability between the two terms must in a certain way veil itself." All of this because of the Infinite.

But the Infinite implies something else as well, and here I come to my second point. If God is infinite, He includes everything and excludes nothing. All possibilities are comprised within Him. Now we describe things as possible in two different senses. The term may refer, on the one hand, to something that is strictly contingent, which may either exist or not exist depending upon conditions beyond its control, and in this sense, possibility is the very opposite of necessity. On the other hand, possibility can mean power or potency, or perhaps fecundity, and this is the meaning which is to be applied to God, for He is at once "both absolute Necessity and infinite Possibility; in the first respect, He transcends everything that is merely possible"—everything contingent or relative—"whereas, in the second respect, He is, not a given possibility of course, since He is absolutely necessary, but Possibility as such." In other words, God "is the Source of all that can be."

At this point, however, a great mystery intrudes. God is also the Source, indirectly and paradoxically, of something that cannot be—namely, nothing. I realize that this will sound very odd. Nevertheless, however strange, the idea follows ineluctably from the Divine infinity. Since nothing can be done which exceeds the limits of the Infinite, this too is done. Nothing is also accomplished to the measure it can be. "Divine Reality would not be what it is unless it included the paradoxical dimension of a kind of tendency towards a nothingness which obviously is never attained."

If you find this to be the biggest puzzle yet, do not be surprised. Our teachers are themselves agreed that "nothingness is the one enigma of metaphysics," far more mysterious than the Supreme Reality itself. But the mystery cannot be denied, either metaphysically or conceptually. Metaphysically, it results from the fact that "All-Possibility must by definition and on pain of contradiction include its own impossibility." We could put the matter in other words by saying that "the infinitude of Reality implies the possibility of its own negation." Conceptually the teaching makes sense because we are in fact able to conceive the idea of nothingness. Were nothing really nothing-at-all, we would not be able to think about it. And yet we do. I know what you mean, for example, when you tell me that there is nothing in the pantry to eat, and a teacher is able to record absences when students miss his class. What we take note of is not of course "nothingness pure and simple," but "its existential effects." We see an image of this in cold which, though it is only a privation or absence of heat, nevertheless "transforms water into snow and ice, as if it had the power to produce bodies." Nothingness certainly has no being or existence of its own, "but it is nonetheless a kind of metaphysical 'direction,' something we can conceive and pursue, but never attain." Its reality is "the quite indirect one of a point of reference."

The Infinite thus contains the possibility of nothingness, the possibility of its own negation. But the Infinite is also the Absolute, and as we have seen, the Absolute is that which cannot not be. Negation is therefore "impossible in the Absolute itself." Hence the only way for God to realize this enigmatic possibility is outside Himself. But how can this be? Since God is infinite, there is nothing outside Him—nowhere else for Him to go. What is God to do? (Please understand that in putting things this way, as if God were faced with some great dilemma, I mean to provoke your thinking. It goes without saying that the anthropomorphism implicit in such questions is altogether inappropriate to the metaphysical Principle. The Supreme Reality is what it is. We must not imagine that it contains unresolved tensions or that it has to go seeking solutions. Let us remember as always the limits of language.)

Since nothingness is not allowed within God Himself, "it is necessary that this 'possibility of the impossible' should be realized in an 'internal dimension' which is 'neither real nor unreal.'" Here we circle back to the idea of *Maya* or the relative. "In a certain sense, *Maya*

represents the possibility for Being of not being." What is it that is
neither real nor unreal? What do we call such a thing? We call it an
illusion, and this as you will recall is one of the meanings of *Maya*.
An illusion, unlike a hallucination, comes about when we see something real, but not in its proper or original form. Since the Supreme
Reality is necessary and cannot not be, it can only seem not to be,
and this is accomplished by the illusion of *Maya*.

God veils Himself, as if He were not, under the cloak of Existence.
This is why "the world is antinomic by definition, which is a way of
saying it is not God." For within the world, "every image is at the
same time true and false." The images are true or real insofar as they
are images of God, but they are false or unreal insofar as they are
just images. At the same time, their very falseness or unreality, to
the extent that it is apprehended as such, is also paradoxically
God—precisely because the Infinite allows Him as it were not to be.
"Reality has entered into nothingness, so that nothingness might
become real."

Before bringing this meditation to a close, I would like to draw
your attention to one final, very important matter. With the idea of
illusion or *Maya*, we have before us a key to solving the so-called
problem of evil. In my experience, there is no more common cause of
religious disbelief in our day than the seeming injustice of suffering.
I am speaking about allegedly rational causes, of course. The spiritual maladies which are at the root of all disbelief are another issue
completely. These deeper problems, however, often manifest themselves in sophistical critiques and arguments, and it is useful to
know how to respond to them on their own level. As I explained earlier, a truly effective spiritual teaching must begin by taking the
skeptic's criticisms into consideration. Here we have an opportunity
to address yet another of the supposed reasons for doubt.

One is often asked why a good, wise, and all-powerful God would
permit the existence of evil. If there is evil, and no one doubts that
there is, it seems that such a God must not exist. But as the perennial philosopher sees it, those who would blame God for the existence of evil have simply never faced up to what it means to exist
within the total metaphysical context that we have been describing.
They fail to see that "to exist means to be other than God, and so to
be bad." They have not grasped the fact that "evil is none other than
'nothingness manifested' or 'the impossible made possible.'" It is the
name given in the formal domain of Manifestation, whether on the

animic or corporal levels, to "those privative manifestations—or 'existentiations of nothingness'"—that come about as the inevitable corollaries of cosmic illusion, the result in turn of the Divine infinitude. It is as if the critic wished to blame the world for not being God, or Manifestation for not being the Principle. We are to be reminded instead of the words of Christ. There is none good but one, that is God, and it must needs be that offenses come.

If God is the only true Good, if He alone is Perfection, then what is not God cannot but be evil, evil being understood as imperfection and not in an ethical or juridical sense. In other words, "the root of all evil is the ontological distance between the world and God, a distance which cannot but exist since God is infinite." Evil is the name which we give to the remoteness of things from the Supreme Reality, and it must manifest itself "in such measure as the world is relatively real." As long as we are subject to the categories of existence, there is no reason to be surprised or puzzled by imperfection.

A concluding caution, however. None of this is meant to provide an excuse for the all too fashionable moral relativism of our day. On the contrary, to say that evil as such is metaphysically necessary is not at all the same thing as averring that such and such an evil is existentially justified. "Assuredly it can be said that the Divinity is 'beyond good and evil,' but on condition of adding that this 'beyond' is in its turn a 'good' in the sense that it testifies to an Essence in which there could be no shadow of limitation." Both good and evil are manifestations of the Principle, but in the one case by affirmation and in the other by privation, and while the opposition between them is transcended in God, they are not to be confused at the level of the world. Offenses must come. But woe to the man by whom they come. Do not forget that the degrees of Reality are degrees of Reality. No level is without any reality at all, and insofar as we live on a particular level, and amidst its conditions, we must treat it seriously, for only thus can it be overcome. Our world may be unreal, but then so are we.

"A mountain is a mountain and not a dream, even for an ant, or it would be in the void that ants would be crossing rocks and climbing slopes."

✤ Chapter 7 ✤

The Open Door

God has opened a door in the middle of creation, and this
open door of the world towards God is man; this opening is
God's invitation to look towards Him, to tend towards Him,
to persevere with regard to Him, and to return to Him.

I come to the last of my meditations on Truth or metaphysical doctrine. Not that we have even come close to exhausting this inexhaustible subject. These few reflections are just the beginning, the least of leading thoughts. But perhaps they will serve to point your way forward toward the actual living of the spiritual life. Theory, after all, is for the sake of practice, and doctrine is the foundation of method. With this in mind, I shall soon be turning to the operational side of my answer to your question as we examine what it means to live by the Truth through Virtue, Beauty, and Prayer. If for now we conclude our explorations of metaphysics as such, it is with the awareness that one could "spend a whole lifetime speculating on the suprasensorial and the transcendent." What really matters, however, is the "fixation of spirit and soul in an unthinkable dimension of the Real," and this depends on a "direct understanding and on a grace, not on having reached a certain phase in the unfolding of the doctrine, for this unfolding has logically no end."

47

There is one final subject, however, that must not be neglected. My aim has been to map out the context of the spiritual journey, and this has meant giving you some sense of the scope and structure of Reality as a whole. But this map would be virtually useless unless we added a first sketch of the human being. It is like those maps one finds in parks or forests, with the arrow indicating where you are at the moment. Metaphysically speaking, where we are is in the human state, and we need to see what this means, how it looks, from the standpoint of the whole. "Before laying down the law as to man's needs and the remedies they require, it is necessary to know what man is; it is necessary to envisage the human being in his totality, or not be concerned with him at all." We already know, of course, that we are not Divine, but neither are we merely animals. This initial sense of ourselves as beings between is the essential key to our nature, and it will be a question of filling in the details.

"The ambiguity of the human state is that we are as it were suspended between God—our Essence—and the human form, which is 'made of clay'; we are so to speak a mixture of divinity and dust." We are indeed beings between, but at the same time our nature includes the extremes which define this middle ground. Neither God nor lifeless matter, man is nevertheless somehow both, for in him all the many degrees of Reality are projected and mirrored. This is what is meant when the perennial philosopher tells us that "there is nothing in the macrocosm that does not derive from the metacosm and which is not to be found again in the microcosm." We have had occasion before to investigate the first half of this maxim. All the levels of the universe, the macrocosm, come about through the radiation or manifestation of God, the metacosm. But all of these levels are to be found as well within each human being, who is himself a microcosm or miniature universe. Hence "to know the nature of subjectivity is to know the structure of the world." The sacred science of *gnosis* need not depend upon arguments from authority. It is there to be read in the script of the human substance itself.

We find ourselves between two poles which are yet within us, and this means that the human state involves both ambiguity, on the one hand, and certain unique prerogatives and responsibilities, on the other. The ambiguity is perhaps easier to discern. We have already taken note of its metaphysical background: "That we are conformed to God—'made in His image'—this is certain; otherwise we would not exist. That we are contrary to God, this also is certain; otherwise we would not be different from God. Without analogy with God we would be nothing. Without opposition to God we would be God."

I know that I am a creature of flesh and blood, caught in a web of conditions that I did not devise, and subject to forces beyond my control. But at the same time, it is not without significance that I do in fact know this, for to the extent that I do, I am obviously something more than this creature alone. If I were completely finite or completely relative, I could have no concept of finitude or relativity, much less apply such an idea to myself. Finitude means boundary or limit. But a limit has meaning only to one who is aware that it has two sides, and who has at least peeked across. Such reflections, of course, serve only to confirm the familiar tensions of our daily existence, which even the most unreflective man has no reason to deny. Who has not experienced the tug of war between spirit and flesh, between the demands of conscience and the desires of the moment? "Man is by definition situated between an intellection which connects him to God and a world which has the power to detach him from God."

Attention was directed earlier to the Intellect, man's connection with the Divine. Here we must look more closely at his connection with the world. The term of choice in this case is *ego*. The word means simply *I* in Latin, but we shall use it to designate the human self understood as an object of consciousness. In other words, the ego is not the elusive Subject whom we spoke about earlier, but that Subject objectified and individualized. The ego is not *I* but *me*. To be more precise, as the esoterist uses the term, the ego includes both the tendency toward objectivation and its result. It is the name both for a centrifugal force, which would draw us away from our central Essence, and for the resulting circumference or particular ego. The former is the "ego as such," and the latter is "such and such an ego." The particular ego is often referred to as the "empirical ego," but be careful that the adjective does not mislead you. More than the physical body or "outer ego," this term refers also to the soul or "inner ego"—that is, all of the psychic qualities and contents of consciousness which characterize an individual man. My talents and temperament, my moods, desires, and memories, my thoughts at this moment—all these are aspects of the empirical ego, all the result of an outwardly directed movement or descensional tendency from God toward the world. "When man turns away from his Divine Essence, his ego becomes like a stone pulling him downwards, and his

Essence turns away from him; what then fills this vacuum is the dark essence, that of formal compression and of the fall."

The idea of a fall needs some elaboration, however. Fall suggests movement between points, but in this case, the points are actually the result of the movement. So intimately are the ego and the world interwoven with each other that there would be no world as we know it into which the ego could fall were it not for the ego, and there would be no ego to do the falling were it not for this world. "The ego is empirically a dream in which we ourselves dream ourselves; the contents of this dream, drawn from our surroundings, are at bottom only pretexts, for the ego desires only its own life." To return to the preceding distinction, the dreamer is the ego as such, and the dream is the empirical ego. "Whatever we may dream, our dream is always only a symbol for the ego which wishes to affirm itself, a mirror that we hold before the 'I' and which reverberates its life in multiple fashions." What man sees in the mirror is a combination of tendencies and images. The first come from himself, and the second come directly from the world: directly, I say, because indirectly they too are produced by the ego. "As we exteriorize ourselves, we create a world in the image of our dream, and the dream thus objectivized flows back upon us, and so on and on, until we are enclosed in a tissue, sometimes inextricable, of dreams exteriorized or materialized and of materializations interiorized."

The world in this case is not simply our spatial environment. It includes the context or framework in which the ego lives, whether external and physical or internal and psychic. But it also involves a temporal dimension and thus the movement or flow of our life from moment to moment. Space and time are both reflections of the ego. Turned as it is on itself, "the ego is ignorance of what is 'the other,'" and "what is time, if not ignorance of what will be 'after,' and what is space if not ignorance of what escapes our sense?" This is why it can be said that "the ego is at the same time a system of images and a cycle; it is something like a museum, and a unique and irreversible journey through that museum." Certain theological formulations would have it that our ignorance has come about as a result of our being fallen creatures, while the skeptic will say that it comes from the unavoidable empirical limits of our senses. But the metaphysician asks us to push deeper. We are to see that ignorance is the cause not the consequence of limitation and fallenness, while it in turn is caused by the ego. "The fundamental cause of illusion and ignorance is not our state of fall nor some deficiency of the existential substance, but the principle of objectification, by which the pole 'being' is cut off from the pure Subject."

Ambiguity, however, is not all that we are. Our ignorance is not the whole Truth. We are obliged to return to the earlier paradox. If I were utterly ignorant, I would never come to know it. If I were completely conditioned by the world that I have manufactured for myself, I would have no vantage point from which to survey my conditioning, nor any leverage with which to raise that world up as an object for inspection. It simply must be the case that *I* am more than *me*. And the moment I realize this, I see that there is more than ambiguity in being human. I become aware of the tremendous prerogatives and responsibilities that devolve upon me as a man.

"Man marks, for the terrestrial world that is his, a limit of the 'creative ray'; man's sufficient cause is being this limit, providing a stop, after the manner of an echo or a mirror, to the 'ray of exteriorization' of the Self." As human beings, you and I are like everything else in Existence, a part of the creative ray of Manifestation, the radiation of the Principle. But insofar as we see this, and are able to distinguish between the Principle and its radiation and to discern the Principle in Manifestation, we are unlike everything else in the ray. Our discernment turns everything around, allowing for a recapitulation or return to God. It is the Self or supra-ontological Subject which acts at the center of our knowing. In order to know what is, we must be what knows. And it is thus that "the human state is a gate of exit—and the only gate for the terrestrial world—not merely out of this world or the formal cosmos, but even out of the immense and numberless objectification that is universal Existence." Woven into the world, we are yet more than that world, and we may thus act as doors through which all of creation can pass on its return to God.

We may act as doors. It is not that we necessarily will. This is a critical point, closely connected to my warning at the end of the last chapter about the seriousness with which we should consider the world. There are no guarantees that a man will live up to the precious opportunity which the human condition affords. We can turn our backs on our vocation. Although the Kingdom of God is within us, the talents we are given may yet be buried. "The prerogative of the human state is objectivity." But here, too, we encounter a paradox. The very same privilege that accounts for our knowledge, and thus for the possibility of return on the plane of the intelligence, is also the basis of our freedom, the basis for a possible refusal on the plane of the will. Man is made an open door, but he may fail to take advantage of the exit, and "the door closes at death when it has been scorned during life." You and I have been given "a rare and precious possibility," but this is coupled with an equally unique responsibility. Truly to understand what it means to be human is to understand "why there is damnation, for he who has refused to pass through the door will never afterwards be able to cross its threshold."

Man alone in this world can undertake the spiritual journey. It is good that you have begun. But you must persevere.

Virtue

Whoso knoweth his soul knoweth his Lord.

—*Muhammad*

Virtue

✧ Chapter 8 ✧

Conforming to God

Knowledge saves us only on condition that it engages all that
we are: only when it constitutes a way which works and
transforms, and which wounds our nature as the plough
wounds the soil.

*W*e come now to the second of the essentials of the spiritual
life. As we do so, it might be helpful to think back to a picture that I sketched in the Introduction. Spirituality is a matter of
reunion with God, and this reunion may be seen as a movement
from where we are to where we should be. Considered from the perspective of *gnosis*, it is a progress or journey toward the Truth—from
the illusions of the ego through the Intellect toward the Supreme
Reality. This same Truth must be present at our starting point, too,
in the form of a theory or doctrine which points us in the right direction, and this is why I began with the preceding metaphysical synthesis. But it is important to remember that Truth comes both at the
start of the race and at the finish line. It is at once our motive and
our prize.

Like every journey, the spiritual quest takes place in a space.
There must be ample room for our progress. If there are obstacles in
the path, they will have to be circumvented or pushed out of the way
in order for movement to be possible. If our motion is sufficiently

forceful, of course, it can itself help to clear the way, pushing aside obstructions by its inherent power, and from this point of view, our motion or movement comes before and creates the space in which we travel. Prayer, I have said, is our movement toward God. If Truth is both the goal and the point of departure, both the target and the bow, Prayer is the arrow, and if shot with sufficient force, this arrow can pierce anything, making its unerring way through the greatest barriers. In this sense, Prayer can open up its own space and fashion a suitable context for itself without our having to make special provisions in advance. Understood in this way, Prayer would actually come next in my list of essentials.

But what if our motion is halting or weak? What if we do not yet have the strength to stretch our bows far enough? What are we to do if we have never prayed before and seem unable to get started? In such a case, we need to talk first about the space through which we are to pass, and then we can turn with greater profit to the passage itself. As I explained earlier, this space is constituted by two things in the spiritual life, one of them internal and the other external. There must be ample room for breathing the breath of Prayer both within our souls and in the ambience or environment which exists around us. The external environment is a matter of Beauty, and we are going to be looking at this constitutive element later. Before doing so, however, I want to spend some time meditating on the inward space of the soul, and hence on the essential called Virtue. In the meantime, Prayer itself need not be postponed. If we save the topic for later, this is not to imply that the reality should be neglected. Even the simplest request for God's help can even now begin assisting you as it "loosens psychic knots or, in other words, dissolves subconscious coagulations and drains away many secret poisons."

The specific path we have undertaken to follow is the path of *gnosis*. I noted some of the reasons for this choice in the first part of the book and have tried to anticipate common objections and to guard against certain misunderstandings. If nothing else, we should have learned that when speaking about knowledge in the spiritual life, something more is intended than mere cerebration. The distinction between the Intellect and the reason helped to underscore this fact. Metaphysical Truth is not to be grasped by thinking alone. Such Truth is given to the heart, not produced by the brain. Of course, the brain is inevitably brought into play when we endeavor to express the knowledge gained by intellection. But thinking should not be considered the source of that knowledge.

Nor can the head alone properly assimilate or cultivate *gnosis.* Once it is given, Truth demands more than just reason if we mean to maintain it. However valid the ideas we have been examining thus far, they will take "their revenge on anyone who limits himself to thinking of them," and this is why "the presence in our mind of metaphysical Truth is by itself inoperative so far as our final ends are concerned." When we are warned against being spoiled by philosophy and vain deceit, it is precisely for this reason. Quite apart from the many erroneous fabrications of man, even true doctrine—orthodoxy—can become a vanity if it takes the form of a logical system alone. "He whose being is too exclusively anchored to thought, he who wants to realize everything in his mind but only succeeds in exhausting virtualities of knowledge, such a man finally slips into error even if he was not in error already, just as the ascending curve of a circle changes imperceptibly to a descending curve." This explains why the traditional promulgation of doctrine always takes place within the protective framework supplied by ritual and sacrament, and why it is directed to those who have prepared themselves in a more than mental way. For "intelligence and metaphysical certainty alone do not save, and do not of themselves prevent titanic falls."

Comprehension of God and conformation to God must go hand in hand. Man must not only seek to know the Truth. He must strive to live fully in accordance with it. I say that he *must,* but I need to be careful here that moralism does not replace metaphysics. We are referring as always to the nature of things, to the fact in this case that comprehension and conformation are naturally two sides of one coin. If we would know God, we must live according to the Divine pattern, not in the sense of yielding to some extrinsic demand—as if we were being shamed into obedience by the pressure of celestial legislation—but simply because such a life will prove to be a lens through which we can see Reality with more and more clarity. To change the metaphor, we are meant to be mirrors, and our actions are to be reflections of Being. We strive to conform ourselves to God simply because God is the Truth we would know. As we discovered in our meditation on the Subject or Self, if man would know what is, he must be what knows.

The name for this conformation is Virtue. In the explorations that follow, I shall be directing your attention to the metaphysical and esoteric significance of Virtue, and we shall look at certain particular virtues which are stressed by the spiritual teacher. My aim in the remainder of this opening chapter is simply to emphasize the importance of Virtue for the actualization or realization of knowledge. You must understand, in short, that "every virtue is an eye that sees God."

Virtue assists in the deepening of our comprehension of doctrine by adding a new dimension to what we already know. "Intelligence that is not accompanied by virtues gives rise to a planimetric knowledge: it is as if one were to grasp but the circle or the square, and not the sphere or the cube." To take just a single example: thinking about God's impassibility is one thing, and none too difficult. But it is something quite different, and not so easy, to live impassibly oneself through the practice of patience and detachment. The man who undertakes to cultivate this particular mode of Divine conformity in his actual day-to-day living is obviously going to understand God better, and be far more in awe of Him, than the man who does not.

At the same time, while giving depth to a knowledge that one already has, Virtue also helps to purify the intelligence so that it might assimilate additional teaching with greater acuteness and subtlety. This is significant because "purity of intelligence is infinitely more important than its actual capacity. 'Blessed are the pure in heart,' said Christ, not 'Blessed are the intelligent.'" Of course, Virtue cannot increase mental power as such. Not every saint is a sage. But as used in this context, intelligence means more than mentation. It includes the discursive mind or reason, but it also comprises imagination and intuition. How quick or retentive our minds happen to be will not necessarily be changed by our efforts to live in accordance with Truth. But such efforts can open up the imaginative and intuitive powers in ways which more than compensate for other weaknesses or flaws. "He who wants to know with the heart-intellect must 'know' with the whole soul, and this implies the purification of the soul and therefore the virtues."

In any case, whatever the specific faculties we might wish to list, to point to the importance of Virtue is to remember that man is a microcosm, a little universe. If the spiritual life is to be complete, it must embrace every part of this universe, for man is much more than a knower alone. This does not mean that Virtue is necessary for knowledge as such. A bad man can still understand that two and two make four. We are not saying that the "Intellect is insufficient and has need of extrinsic help." The Intellect or intuitive power remains infallible, and its knowledge is in need of nothing, even virtuous living. This is why I said earlier that knowledge is its own proof and guarantee. Nevertheless "man is not the Intellect." Uncreated and uncreatable, the Intellect is greater than he is. If he means to assimilate what the Intellect shows him, his individuality must be modified and brought into line. If it is not, the "absence of Virtue can lead, in one degree or another, to a split between man and his intelligence: man can be the infallible mouthpiece of the Spirit, but the relationship between the one and the other is a grace"—the "static and innate" grace of intellection precisely.

Grace, you may be thinking, is the opposite of human effort, for grace means unmerited gift. And yet like all of God's gifts, the grace of knowledge must be freely accepted. "The intellective center of a being is not reached without involving his volitional circumference." Grace requires a climate in which it might flourish. Hence "he who possesses Truth must none the less merit it, although it is a free gift. Truth is immutable in itself, but in us it lives, because we live. If we want the Truth to live in us, we must live in it." And we must live in it fully. Every part of our lives must become integrated into the spiritual journey, for the Truth, being God, is total. "To know God with all that we are: the very infinity of the object of knowledge requires the totality of the act of knowing, and this totality requires the essential virtues." I am not only a mind which can think. I am a soul which can love and a will which can choose. And it is only when my loving and obedient choosing are brought into line with my thinking that I become an adequate vehicle for the Supreme Reality. "Knowledge of the Total demands on man's part totality of knowing. It demands, beyond our thought, all our being, for thought is a part, not the whole; and this indicates the goal of the spiritual life." As we shall see later, even the body needs to be involved at some point and on some level in this full commitment of the complete human being. For "he who conceives the Absolute—or who believes in God—cannot stop short *de jure* at this knowledge, or at this belief, realized by thought alone; he must on the contrary integrate all that he is into his adherence to the Real, as is demanded precisely by its absoluteness and infinitude." Although not every saint is a sage, every sage is a saint.

I must conclude with an important qualification. The impression has perhaps been given that Virtue is of a strictly instrumental significance. It is certainly correct to say that Virtue "necessarily opens onto wholeness of mind, hence onto knowledge of the Real," but you must not suppose that the virtues are merely means to this end. They are instead irreplaceable goods in their own right—facets of the gem of Divinity, inward lights of the soul by which it participates in the attributes and powers of God. When "realized to their very limit—as far as their universal and Divine prototypes"—the virtues "coincide with metaphysical truths." They do not simply lead to such truths, or apply such truths. They are these truths, "concrete, seen, and lived." We should therefore beware of "considering virtues only in relation to their 'technical' utility and not in relation to their Beauty."

Beauty of soul simply is what it is, the inward space of the Real.

✢ Chapter 9 ✢

Perfection and Anonymity

Every man likes to be out in the light and fresh air; no one would like to be shut up in a dark, airless tower; and that is how one should love the virtues, and detest the vices.

*T*he esoterist means to go straight to the heart of things, and when it comes to the subject of Virtue, his procedure is no different. He wishes to teach us the essentials, to disentangle our thinking from all the irrelevancies and pettiness with which human action is so often encumbered, and which can paralyze the will of even the best intentioned man. Please do not go looking in these meditations for a casuistical treatment of specific ethical issues. You will find here no musings about the various moral dilemmas of our day, nor any attempt to repeat or compete with the commandments and precepts of the great religions, still perfectly sufficient for those willing to live by them. What you will find instead are keys to the simplicity of soul that is needed if we wish to act wisely in all situations.

In spite of such great promise, however, an esoteric understanding of Virtue is going to seem inadmissible to a number of people, owing in large part to this very simplicity. Complication can be very convenient after all. If we could but convince ourselves that the world is a hopelessly tangled place and that human life is merely a movement from one insoluble dilemma to another, then there would

61

be no reason to feel guilty when we fail to be good. You are familiar with this all too common psychological strategy, and you will have doubtless been exposed to the moral relativism which is its philosophical counterpart and which provides such a convenient theoretical justification for the practice of vice. If ethics are a matter of social convention—if there is no single standard of objective and universal goodness, but only a multitude of subjective and particular preferences—then there is nothing to stand in the way of identifying my responsibilities with my desires. Nor is there anything to stop me from creating a new kind of religion or spirituality for myself through an inversion or perversion of language. Simplicity in such a case comes to mean going with the flow of my passions and doing whatever I wish at the moment, while complexity is the result of too many burdensome rules.

I hope in this section to describe the place and purpose of true simplicity and to explain if I can the perennial philosopher's approach to the virtues. But I shall not be addressing the relativists as such. For one thing, I have in mind as always your particular question, and it seems to me that if you yourself were just looking for excuses, you would not have wanted to embark on the spiritual path in the first place, or not at least the path of knowledge. As for those who may read these remarks and who persist in denying the existence of moral absolutes, they need only look back to our meditations on Truth. Ample clues were provided there for disposing of relativism and subjectivism in all their forms.

I have in mind a different audience now, one which may be resistant to esoterism for quite another reason—not because they believe there is no such thing as sin or vice, and not because they find life too confusing and cloudy to determine the difference between good and evil. I am thinking instead of certain of the religious faithful I know who not only believe in the existence of sin, but who insist that man as such is sin—that man as we know him is by definition a sinner, who can do nothing to save himself. A metaphysical exposition of the meaning of Virtue is going to be something of a scandal to such people, and I would like to go on record at once with an acknowledgment of that fact, and with a promise to give their position its due. I have no intention of compromising or altering what the metaphysician has to say on this subject. But at the same time by putting his doctrine in its proper context, I hope to help believers of good will appreciate its importance and value.

They will need to listen carefully, however, lest true *gnosis* be confused with its counterfeits. There is abroad today a specious and very dangerous brand of spirituality promulgated by those who have rejected the wisdom of their fathers and who would have us believe that each individual is his own potential deity. Such people are not above distorting traditional religious language and concealing their relativism under a cloak of spiritual terms. We are living in a new age, it is said, with altogether different needs and possibilities. Man has grown up and is called to take charge of the universe, whose very future depends in some way upon the evolution and actualization of the human spirit. This evolution, moreover, each of us must superintend for himself, for no two individuals are alike, and no one should impose his own beliefs on someone else.

At first—but only at first if one is paying attention—it may seem as if the perennial philosopher is saying something similar. He teaches that "the fall of man as such could not be total," and that Virtue consists essentially therefore in fidelity to our "fundamental being" or "theomorphic nature" since there remains within every man a level of "primordial perfection" existing on an inward plane "deeper than the level of the fall." Hence Virtue is not something which I do or acquire. Virtue is what I already am in my transpersonal depths. But here precisely is where we must exercise caution. Here is where authentic *gnosis* may begin sounding to certain *bhaktas* too much like the historical deviation of gnosticism. Has the metaphysician forgotten that apart from God there can be no salvation? Are his claims not a presumptuous inflation of the creature? Is man his own god, and is the way of knowledge to be a path of spiritual narcissism?

The answer to all these questions is an emphatic and resounding negative. But to see why, we have to listen to both sides of the doctrine of Virtue. As usual, esoteric teaching is not without a dimension of paradox. Virtue is indeed what I am. But the true esoterist is the first to remind us that what I am is not mine. All we possess, beginning with our very existence, is pure gift, and whatever Virtue can be found within us is merely borrowed. There exists within man a primordial level of perfection unaffected by what certain traditions call original sin, but this level must not be confused—as it always is in the counterfeit doctrines—with human individuality, for the particular person is indeed "fallen and sinful." Think back to our discussion of the human creature as a being poised between two levels of reality, between divinity and dust, and recall the very important distinction between *I* and *me*. When our teachers speak about "the quasi-divine character of man," they do not want us to forget in the meantime "the great Gospel virtues—charity, humility, poverty, childlikeness"—which "represent so many negations of that ontological 'bubble' which is the ego." It is true that Virtue is what we already are, for "God has put into our substance all the virtues; they derive from the nature of our substance, and this nature is primordial worship." But at the same time, "a virtue is never an acquisition or a property: it always belongs to God, and through Him to the *Logos;* our concern must be to eliminate whatever is opposed to the virtues, not to gain virtues for ourselves; we must give free passage to the Sovereign Good."

As always, the background for this perspective is the nature of things, rooted in the Supreme Reality. We must therefore return to the basics: God alone is, and what is, is God. God is both beyond everything and within everything, at once Absolute and Infinite, and in our efforts to be faithful to both of these Divine dimensions, a middle way is necessary. Early in our meditations on Truth, this path led us between the extremes of rationalism and fideism, between too much logic and too little logic. Here the same path requires that we avoid both the contemporary and very popular cult of the individual, on the one hand, and certain religious opinions concerning the totality of the fall, on the other—both too little sin, as it were, and too much. I should add, however, that if one had to choose, it would be better to err with the latter, with those who believe that we are utterly sinful, just as it is better to be a fideist than a rationalist. The perennial philosophy always sides with the religious traditions, even with their pious excesses, whenever a choice is presented between them and the profane and worldly thinking of the skeptic or critic. It is on their side even when they imagine themselves to be opposed to it.

The opposition of the pious stems in this case from the metaphysician's claim that man is intrinsically or fundamentally perfect. But if God is infinite, as no believer will deny, the logic of this teaching is indisputable. For the Infinite cannot but be immanent, in us as in all things, and from this it follows that Virtue consists in "maintaining the soul in the virginity of our fundamental being." The esoterist "sees Virtue, not in human initiatives, but in an existential quality, namely the primordial and innocent nature of creation." Everything is a manifestation of God in some form or some mode. If it were not, it would simply not be. God's perfection is thus to be found wherever one looks, and all the more so in the being of man, who is made in His image. Hence one may say that "the return to God is inherent in the fact of existence: our being itself offers the way of return, for that being is Divine in its nature, otherwise it would be nothing; that is why we must return, passing through the strata of our ontological reality, all the way to pure Substance, which is one."

None of this is to deny, however, the indispensable, complementary truth of transcendence. As absolute, God is the only Reality, and He is therefore the only good. It may be true that "fallen man is not all of man," but man is in fact fallen. To be sure, the metaphysician interprets this fact differently from the *bhakta*. Rather than putting the matter in juridical or legal terms and picturing us as criminals before the Divine tribunal, he says instead that "the fall was precisely the rupture between reason and Intellect, the ego and the Self." And yet he has no doubt that this rupture "involves the human species" as a whole, and that if the fall essentially is "nothing other than the reaction of reality" to man's willing delusion, this reaction is no less total and all-encompassing. "The sense of sin is really the consciousness of an equilibrium that surpasses our personal will." It is therefore inseparable from the sense of the sacred, which is an "instinct for that which surpasses us and which, for that reason, must not be touched by ignorant and iconoclastic hands." In other words, an awareness of sin is the inevitable corollary of a true knowledge of God. In the face of the Absolute, existence by definition is sinful. All have sinned and fallen short of the glory of God.

It follows that our virtues are simply on loan. "The accident of human virtue cannot be a production of the creature, and this is precisely why the qualities or talents of a man are called 'gifts.' Pride is believing that we make a present of our virtues to God." We are mere relativities, and "we necessarily possess in a relative manner that which God has bestowed upon us, and which He alone possesses in an absolute manner." The Divine infinitude and immanence lead to the same admission. Since God is everywhere, all things are in God, and the result is that "no value can be situated outside the Sovereign Good." All goods, all beauties, all truths are contained in that which is supremely good, supremely beautiful, and supremely true. Therefore, "one could say that man enters into Virtue as he would enter into a sanctuary, and that Virtue expels the ambitious who claim it for themselves." Even though a man be a saint, he is obliged to respect the "anonymity of the virtues," to admit that "only our faults belong to us; our qualities belong to God."

I hope you can see why the claim to perfection is in no sense intended as an exaltation of the individual ego. In fact, both anonymity and primordial perfection guard against the ego's subtle efforts to extend its scope. By comparing myself to an external standard, even if it be the standard of God's own law, and however humiliating the comparison may be, I inevitably end up perpetuating my individuality and interposing it as a kind of screen between myself and God. It is with this in mind that *"gnosis* objectifies sin—error carried into action—by referring it back to its impersonal causes," unlike the "moral perspective" of the religious believer which "subjectifies the act by identifying it as it were with the agent." In other words, the metaphysician attributes sin to our tendency toward objectification, which is the ego as such, and this is done in order to prevent a given ego from trying to take too much credit for its fallenness. "That alone is immoral in itself which is contrary to pure Truth and to human nature as such," and thus any individual agent, however ethically just his deeds, is immoral precisely insofar as he thinks himself independently real. When we say, therefore, that esoterism "goes right to the existential roots of the virtues," finding them "beyond moral effort in the nature of things," or that the perfect is that which is "rooted in existence, not that which depends on action," we mean by this strategy to circumvent everything that divides us from the immanent Self, who alone is perfect, and this includes the idea that good works and virtues are something to be added to our being. In fact they are that being, beyond all individuality, were we only to see it.

When it comes to the actual living of the virtuous life, we must therefore realize that "the desire to vanquish faults because it is 'I' who have them is ineffectual, since it falls within the same category as the faults themselves." We should instead "tend towards perfection because we understand it and therefore love it, and not because we desire that our ego should be perfect." If we would tend toward perfection without this movement itself turning into yet another obstacle, then we are going to have to admit that Virtue is something simple, direct, immediate, and natural. I shall endeavor to describe these qualities as we look at specific virtues in the meditations following.

Just as Truth is what the intelligence knows when it simply looks, so Virtue is what the soul feels when it simply loves. It is what we are because it is that which is.

✤ Chapter 10 ✤

Humility

Christ was humiliated on the cross through identifying Himself, in the night of abandonment, with the night of the human ego, and not through identifying Himself with such and such an "I."

*I*t is time to take a look at specific virtues. While Virtue is fundamentally a state of being and not a deed or an act, it is nevertheless "able to assume, according to circumstances, an aspect of volitive affirmation, hence of exteriorization and activity." We are not to think of Virtue in the singular as if it were the result of virtues in the plural, nor should virtues in the plural be measured by meritorious actions. And yet Virtue is expressed through the virtues, and these virtues are manifested by one's actions. Conformation to God is nothing other than the primordial perfection of human nature, and this perfection is essentially what we already are. But if we are to become what we are by eliminating the faults standing between us and God, then we need a specific direction to work in. "Intrinsic Virtue lies beyond all moral specification," but in the absence of specificity, we would never reach it. In addition to theory, we therefore need advice about practicing particular virtues, and this advice the perennial philosophy is ready to provide.

The spiritual journey is often divided into three basic stages. It would actually be somewhat more accurate to speak of three dimensions, for like length, breadth, and depth, these three elements build upon each other rather than succeeding each other. The first is purification or purgation. "Every spiritual path begins with an inversion with regard to the preceding state." The soul must be detached from the world, and this means not only giving up certain things, but being stripped or cleansed of all the desires and images which keep us bound to those things even in their absence. Next comes illumination or expansion. Once emptied of its egoistic longing to have and to control, the soul can open out and be filled with the light of true knowledge. It begins to appreciate the beauty and goodness of the creatures around it, rather than looking at them for the sake of acquisition and use, and they cease to be opaque commodities and become instead translucent messages or theophanies. Finally, there is perfection or union, which is the ultimate goal of the spiritual life. We shall be discussing this highest of levels in more detail in our meditations on Prayer. Very briefly for now, perfection has to do with man's full participation in the Divine Essence, though without the Divine Person becoming any less our Creator and Lord. "Man cannot become 'God': the servant cannot change into the Lord; but there is something in the servant that is capable—though not without the Lord's grace—of surpassing the axis 'servant-Lord' or 'subject-object' and of realizing the absolute 'Self.'" More of this later.

I mention these three dimensions at this point because each of them corresponds to a particular virtue. Just as there are three basic parts to the spiritual journey, so there are three fundamental virtues. Each virtue anticipates a degree of advancement in our return to God, and by eliminating what is contrary to those virtues in his soul, a man can prepare himself to go beyond the soul in the grace of perfection. The first of the fundamental virtues, corresponding to purgation, is humility or "the effacing of the ego." The second is charity or "the giving of oneself," corresponding to illumination or expansion. And the third is veracity or objectivity, "the realization of Truth," which anticipates the stage of union. These are "the three 'dimensions' of perfect *gnosis*," coinciding with "the three great stages of the spiritual life." In the remainder of this chapter, I would like to say a few things about humility, turning then to charity and veracity in the next two meditations.

A saint was once asked to list the four most important virtues, and he replied that they were humility, humility, humility, and humility. We had better make certain that we understand something so important. What exactly is humility?

The first point to stress is that humility is not the same thing as an inferiority complex. True humility is something very direct and natural. It means taking stock of your real worth, objectively and impartially, as if you were someone else. It is occasionally twisted, however, into something grotesque, and one comes away thinking that if an intelligent man or a beautiful woman wishes to be humble, he must pretend he is stupid and she must suppose herself ugly. When humility is replaced by false modesty, it cannot but collapse under careful inspection, and those who might otherwise have been attracted to the spiritual life will be confirmed as a result in their cynicism.

In speaking of such distortions, I have in mind a particular style of religious piety which believes that fallen man is essentially sinful—we discussed this before—and which puts its belief into practice through exaggerated self-deprecation and ascetical labors. In order to cut off all pride, the believer confesses himself to be the greatest of sinners, and he looks to suffering as the very heart of spirituality, whether the involuntary suffering which comes from sickness and the other trials of life or suffering voluntarily undertaken as penance. From this point of view, to be humble is to think oneself the worst or most vile of men, and to cultivate humility means inevitable suffering and pain. In the perspective of *gnosis,* however, these associations are individualistic and illogical, and they are therefore obstacles—or at least distractions—to those attempting to follow the way of knowledge. "It is illogical to believe oneself to be 'the worst of men,'" and "this is not only because the worst of men would not take himself to be such, for if he did he would not be the worst, but because such a unique individual as this does not exist, any more than does 'the most beautiful of women'; for if beauty has by definition an infinity of equivalent modes which are reciprocally incomparable, the same is true of every other quality, and also of every vice." Many men cannot all be the worst, and in trying to act as if they were, by dwelling upon the extent of their personal vices, they may all too easily end up exaggerating and reinforcing their egos. Their efforts are comparable to piling fuel on a fire.

The metaphysician certainly admits that "the conviction of being the basest of men may determine a movement towards God; it may open a fissure in our darkness and thus allow grace to flow in. But from a more profound point of view, the question of knowing whether a man is 'high' or 'low' is a matter of complete indifference. What is important to know is that every being, every relativity, is a limitation and thus a 'nothingness.'" Metaphysics "does not admit of subjective positions that are contrary to objective Truth." It is therefore not content with bhaktic definitions of humility, which tend to be "individualistic, sentimental, and penitential" and are "opposed to pride as the color green is opposed to the color red." Such humility is "always an affectation." In its place the esoterist means to put the white light of Truth, for Truth "surpasses every other value, so that to submit to Truth is the best way to be humble." This perspective is based once again on the nature of things and not on "a voluntarist and emotional automatism"—not, in other words, on an understanding of human nature which identifies a man's spiritual state with certain choices, struggles, feelings, or experiences, or which demands of him "an obligatory *mea culpa* that has nothing concrete in view."

Humility for the gnostic is simply self-knowledge. It consists in looking at myself with the same degree of detachment I would have if I were looking at a total stranger. It means considering both my good points and bad and treating myself as severely as the Truth will allow, but not more. The qualification supplied by that last phrase is crucial, for it spells the difference between the advocates of a juridical asceticism on the one hand, who "overlook the fact that men are not all alike," and wayfarers along the path of knowledge on the other hand, who readily acknowledge that "ascesis is useful or necessary for man such as he is in fact, for man excluded from the earthly and heavenly Paradises," but who find that our very existence affords sufficient suffering without our having to go looking for troubles. It is important to recognize that relativity is already insignificant enough without our having to make ourselves even smaller by way of such luxuries as humiliation or abjection.

When someone announces that he is the greatest of sinners, "one would like to paraphrase this expression by saying that he is the man most aware of the hazards of contingency." For humility means seeing myself as I am, seeing the ego for what it is, not simply in relation to other men, but in the face of the Absolute, and this is why true humility always goes hand in hand with the fear of God. What we call humility on the social plane and with a view to modest comportment toward other people is holy fear on the celestial plane and in view of the spiritual journey. And by fear I mean awe. Do not make the common mistake of treating fear and fright as synonyms. Being scared or frightened or anxious is not what we seek. Such emotions are once again of a purely individual order. They are simply the cries of an ego in distress. By contrast, the metaphysician has in mind something deeper, something much closer to dread or wonder. "The fear of God is not in any way a matter of feeling," or not at least feeling alone. It is a function instead of the intelligence, and it "consists in taking account at every moment of a Reality which infinitely surpasses us, against which we can do nothing, in opposition to which we could not live, and from the teeth of which we cannot escape." In the final analysis, humility means knowing that God alone is, and that I am nothing. If "pride is to prefer oneself to God," humility is knowing that there is really nothing but God for a man to prefer. If pride is "that 'something' which prevents man from 'losing his life' for God," humility is what comes from seeing that there was actually no life to lose.

As for the question of asceticism, the esoterist readily agrees that suffering is an important key to one's relationship with God and that "no man can reach perfection without trials." One could even say that "ascesis is an auxiliary" of intellection, at least in certain cases. But rather than looking at particular sufferings as if they came marked with our individual names, and rather than punishing the ego by making it miserable, we are asked to recall instead that manifestation by its very nature is imperfect, and that imperfection means evil and pain. "Since evil is inevitable in the world, it is inevitable also in one's destiny; being necessary in the economy of the objective reality surrounding us, it is no less necessary in the experience of the subject-witness." For this reason, the imperfections of the world cannot but include certain trials and sufferings. The discrepancy or disproportion between God and the world, between the Cause and the effect, "must be manifested in the term which is relative, and that is precisely the meaning of suffering and death." None of this means that we are to become fatalists, of course, or that we should act as if we were simply the passive victims of circumstance and chance. A man may well avoid certain particular evils, and he has a right, even a responsibility, to try. But it is impossible to avoid evil as such, and true humility consists in an unbroken recognition of this fact. Every man must sometimes suffer, and the metaphysical ascetic—if I might use such a phrase—is the person who accepts this condition with resignation. He understands that "the cause of our trials is inscribed in our very relativity," and that "nothing but collective sanctity, which is possible in principle but not in fact, could transform the earth and take us out of a world of cleavages and absurdities."

This knowledge, humbly accepted, becomes in turn the foundation for realization or perfection—for our freedom from the ego and our reunion with the Self. "The cosmic possibility that constitutes the individuality is what it must be, in its limitation as well as in its positive content, and in its possibilities of transcending itself: finite and passible in its contours, it is infinite and impassible in its substance, and this is why trials carry within themselves the virtuality of liberation. They are messengers of a liberty which, in our immutable and immanent reality, has never ceased to be, but which is obscured by the clouds of moving contingency." I spoke earlier about the proofs of God, and among them was the proof *a contrario* supplied by privative phenomena. Suffering provides each of us with a concrete opportunity to make such a proof come alive within the very substance of our being. But if we intend to take advantage of that opportunity, we must be humble enough to realize that things could not be otherwise.

The next time you feel resentful or bitter or would like to complain or whine about the injustice of the universe, ask yourself precisely who it is that is whining, and then remind him that he is getting exactly what he deserves—or more precisely, that he is seeing what he is. The world owes us nothing, but we owe everything to God.

❖ Chapter 11 ❖

Charity

*When man places himself in the neighbor, God places Him-
self in man; to abolish what separates us from the neighbor
is to abolish what separates us from God.*

C harity in our day has been too often equated with the giving of
money or material goods to the poor. When we trace the word
back to its ancient roots, however, we find that it has to do primarily
with an immaterial transaction. Charity is spiritual love. I use the
adjective to distinguish this kind of love from the loves of romance,
friendship, and family—all of them loves which feed the ego, unless
tempered by the selfless love of charity. When I provide something
good for you with no expectation of return or thanks and without
consideration for whether I desire you or like your companionship
or am related to you or have grown accustomed to your habits and
moods, and without even being concerned whether you think that
what I have provided is good, I am practicing the love of charity.
Such love is the second fundamental virtue: a second mode of assim-
ilating the Truth, a second means of drawing near to God, and a second way of becoming what we already are.
    Like all of the virtues, charity pertains to the soul. As you may
have noticed before, *soul* can be used in two distinct ways. If we
think of the human microcosm as including three principal levels,

73

then the soul will refer to the second, middle level: below the human Spirit or Intellect, which corresponds to Beyond-Being, and above the body, which corresponds to Existence. Understood in this way as corresponding to Being, the soul contains everything which can bring us into contact with the Person of God, specifically the mind, the imagination, the feelings or sentiment, the will, and the memory. But *soul* can also be used to designate the feelings or the sentiment in particular. When used in this sense, the soul is understood as a content, not a container, and it is synonymous with the affective dimension of man, as distinct from the intellective and volitive elements. All of the virtues pertain to the soul in the first sense, for they bring into play all of the subtle aspects of man's individuality. But the specific virtue of spiritual love pertains in a unique way to the soul in its second meaning, for the human element of sentiment or feeling is characterized above all by its capacity for charity.

When I talk about feeling, I realize that you may be a little confused. Have we not said that in the perspective of *gnosis*, it is the Truth that counts, and not our likings or dislikings? And did I not just finish explaining in the previous chapter that true humility is objective and impartial—that the perennial philosopher does not base humility on what is merely individualistic and sentimental in a given man's remorse for his sins? It may seem that I am now saying the opposite. For we must now affirm that the virtue of charity involves precisely our feeling or sentiment. Just as affectivity is an essential component of the human state, so is its accommodation to God a necessary part of the spiritual life. Is there an inconsistency here?

A reminder and a distinction should help to clear up this confusion. The reminder is simply that "one must know how to put each thing in its place." Our attention was called to this maxim when we discussed the degrees of Reality, but it is just as relevant here. A sense of proportion is essential at every stage of our journey. To say that something is less important than something else, and that it should therefore not be allowed to assume command, is to put that thing in its place. It is not, however, to pretend that the thing has no place or importance at all. When we say, therefore, that feelings do not determine the *jnani*'s relationship with Heaven, this is to put them in their place, but it is not to imply that man has no feelings or that they should play no role in spirituality. "In the human microcosm, the feeling soul is joined to the discerning Intellect, as in the

Divine Order, Mercy is joined to Omniscience; and as, in the final analysis, Infinitude is consubstantial with the Absolute."

We must make a careful distinction between emotion or sentiment as such and emotionalism or sentimentality. The former is like a window which is open to the world, and which is capable of allowing in the fresh air and light of objective Reality. "Emotion or sentiment is in this case a mode of assimilation; it is thus a subordinate mode of knowledge." But emotionalism is a condition of subjective distortion, where the inward and purely individual state of a given soul becomes an obstacle to its awareness of the world outside. This is something that is obviously to be avoided along the way of knowledge. In pointing to the connection between charity and sentiment, I am certainly not saying that this important virtue should be held hostage by our passing moods or preferences. Quite the contrary, exercising true love will often require that we act against the grain of our desires and aversions, and this demands a sustained effort of will and a persistent struggle against the passions. Spiritual love is not something that we fall into, but something that we must work at.

Feelings understood as wishes, whims, or moods will often get in the way of this work and interfere with our progress. But at the same time, feeling or sentiment can also be considered an organ of perception, as it is for example when the tenor of our soul allows us to experience inwardly the objective difference between the major and minor keys in music or the qualities of certain colors or forms in the plastic arts. In such cases, "emotivity manifests and allows one to perceive those aspects of a good or an evil which mere logical definition could not manifest directly and concretely." Understood in this sense, feeling is important in coming to terms with the principles of metaphysics, for though such principles may appear to some to be purely abstract, they "necessarily confer upon the soul of the knowing subject the sentiment of certitude, and also serenity, peace, and joy." These sentiments are themselves modes of adequation, which can deepen our comprehension of Truth, and which may in turn help to motivate us in practicing the virtues. "True knowledge does not dry up the soul and true charity does not dissolve Truth." Man is not only a head. He also has a chest, and the two are intimately linked. This brings us back to our earlier point about the meaning of Intellect. Intellection is not simply cerebration, I said, for it is rooted in the heart, and the heart is the center of the whole human being. It follows that while "metaphysics is beyond charity," nevertheless "a metaphysician without charity seriously risks compromising the doctrine because of the indirect repercussions of his failing on the workings of his intelligence."

There are two mistakes about love that you will have to avoid if you want to understand its significance in the spiritual life. Both mistakes are very common today. One is thinking that the spiritual life is a purely selfish affair and therefore opposed to love. The other is thinking that love means being soft and gentle. Each of these popular errors results from cutting off charity towards other people, what we might call horizontal love, from the vertical love we are to have for God. Loving God with the whole of our being is the first and great commandment, said Christ, for it alone gives meaning and value to the second commandment, which is that we love our neighbor as ourselves. "Charity is in essence to love God more than ourselves, to love our neighbor as ourselves, thus to love ourselves, but less than God; not to love our neighbor more than ourselves, and not to feel ourselves obliged to give him what, in our opinion, we would not deserve if we were in his place." Let us try to see what this means.

Many of our contemporaries seem to think that the contemplative life is pursued only by those who despise other people, and the hermit or recluse is often held in derision for his supposed misanthropy. This mistake is frequently made by religious believers themselves, whose models of spirituality tend to be drawn from the ranks of philanthropists and other visible helpers, people engaged in charitable works of various kinds: caring for the sick, feeding the hungry, and so forth. But if you think about it, this is clearly shortsighted. Those who equate the spiritual path with selfishness or who suggest that contemplativity is incomplete in itself, requiring as its complement a life of service in the world, have forgotten that "the busy activity of human kind is a very small thing" which can "neither create good nor destroy evil." They appear not to realize that social action as such does "no more than switch around bad things and good." The only act of charity which can have permanent consequences is the act which seeks "to rid the soul of illusions and passions and thus rid the world of a maleficent being; it is to make a void so that God may fill it and, by this fulness, give Himself." The greatest gift of love is the one which has the greatest good in view. But the greatest good is salvation, and mine is the only soul which with God's help I can certainly save. "Since it is impossible that we do to others as much good as we can do to ourselves—sanctity being incommunicable—it would be senseless to love others more than ourselves; a love which does not answer to any objective reality is an empty thing, bound to go astray."

Empty love seems the rule of our times. Appeals to charitable action are common, but they are just as commonly linked with moralistic self-righteousness. Demagogues and social engineers of assorted political persuasions, taking advantage of our culture's prevailing concern for physical comfort and material well-being, deliberately manipulate our feelings of pity and guilt, and the result is that charity is almost exclusively identified with the redistribution of ephemeral goods and power. But "this is merely a defiance hurled at God." Fundamentally it is an attempt "to show that man is better than God, or that man alone is good—man 'despiritualized' and thereby 'dehumanized.'" Please do not misunderstand me. There is obviously nothing wrong with doing good for one's neighbor. All the traditions require it, and the perennial philosopher is quick to point out that material gifts and works of mercy, besides helping other people, are of immeasurable benefit to the giver's own soul. Nevertheless the man whose understanding of charity is strictly confined to this horizontal dimension has failed to realize that his good works, however commendable, contain inevitably "a poison which is eliminated only by the conviction that God has no need of all this."

What God wants, "while wanting nothing of course," is our immortal soul. "In the final analysis, God wants Himself in us. One must therefore beware of any materialistic and demagogic conception of charity and never forget that what 'interests' God—and the sole thing that can 'interest' Him—is the eternal life of him who gives and the eternal life of him who receives." Nor should we forget that these two lives are intimately connected. I have said that sanctity is incommunicable. It is equally true, however, that the holiness of a given man may well attract others to undertake the spiritual journey themselves and to attain by God's grace their own sanctity. "He who is capable of becoming a saint but neglects to become one cannot save anyone; it is hypocrisy pure and simple to hide one's own weakness and lukewarmness behind a screen of good works." Much that would pass for altruism is in fact just another form of egoism.

A second obstacle to understanding true charity is the popular fallacy that love means never causing pain and never feeling anger. Love is equated with softness and tolerance, and tolerance itself, far from meaning that one has agreed to bear the weight of some error or vice, has become tantamount to thinking that there are actually no errors or vices at all. The man who objects to sin is the only real sinner in this scheme, for his so-called dogmatism represents a failure to love. You are familiar with this attitude, I am sure, and as you have almost certainly noticed, it too has infected contemporary religious belief. The faithful seem more and more willing to compromise their traditions in the interest of what they take to be charity, tolerance, and open-mindedness. Here again the problem comes from trying to have the horizontal without the vertical, love of man without love of Truth, and the result is the familiar substitute called being nice.

"To love creatures outside God is as senseless as wishing to enclose the sun's rays in a box," for the creature is relative, and all relativity points beyond itself to the Absolute, upon which it is continuously and entirely dependent for its very existence. In our last meditation, humility was described as seeing ourselves as if we were someone else, and treating ourselves as severely as the Truth will allow, but not more. True charity can be defined as the converse. It is seeing other people as if they were ourselves, and treating them as indulgently as the Truth will allow, but not more. Once again, the concluding qualification is important. To give in to the vices of the neighbor, or to encourage him to think that anything and everything is acceptable provided only that he sincerely wants it, is to assist in cutting him off from his true Source, the one God who is Truth, and this could hardly be called an act of charity. What I am to love in my neighbor is "the potentiality of the Divine presence," and not the constellation of desires and habits and complaints that constitute his ego, for this ego is illusory and impermanent. I am to love my neighbor as myself, and this means that "charity starts from the truth that my neighbor is not other than myself." Recalling what was said about the theophanic phenomenon of consciousness, I am obliged to admit that "in the sight of God," my neighbor "is neither more nor less 'I' than I am myself" and therefore that "what is given to 'another' is given to 'myself.'" In short, "my neighbor is also made in the image of God."

What all of this means, practically speaking, is that "charity or 'compassion' is not flabbiness" and that real love may hate and hurt. It may hate the sin, though not the sinner. Metaphysically, this amounts to hating a given ego and not the ego as such. Indeed true love may in some cases be required to injure the empirical ego, its own above all, as it seeks to be the means of lasting good. Whatever special response might be demanded by a given set of circumstances, love must be solid, and it may need to be hard. For "goodness due to weakness or dreaming is not a virtue; generosity is beautiful to the extent that man is strong and lucid." And this strength cannot but express itself sometimes as anger and indignation. "There is a hatred which is lucid and thus has nothing passional about it, and this is the aversion to our own faults and to what corresponds to them in the world around us." Notice that the force of our anger is to be directed in the first instance toward what is inside of us, and then toward those things in the world outside which are either the effects or the causes of the ego's own maladies. There is no question here of wishing to encourage self-righteousness. The point is simply that "just contempt is both a weapon and a means of protection," and it is a weapon of special importance to those of us who are engaged in spiritual warfare while still living and working in the world. There is certainly also such a thing as dispassion or indifference, but "this is an eremitical attitude that is not necessarily practicable or good in human society." *Maya* is what it must be, and from that point of view, we are all obliged to cultivate a spirit of detachment. But this inward resignation to the play of possibilities in no way excludes knowing that some things are good and others are bad, nor is spiritual indifference inconsistent with our loving the former and hating the latter. "In a spiritual man, there is continuity between his inward impassibility—resulting from the consciousness of the Immutable—and his emotion: when a spiritual man becomes angry, it is so to speak on the basis of his contemplative impassibility and not in a manner contrary to it, whereas a profane man becomes totally enclosed in his anger." Without this distinction of levels, holy wrath would be impossible, "the fulminations of the *Magnificat* or of the Sermon on the Mount would be inexplicable," and Christ would not have cleansed the temple.

Charity is a fundamental virtue, essential to the spiritual life. It is the soul loving God above all, and then loving man, and through these loves seeing, tasting, touching—and finally becoming—the Truth. Intent upon the greatest of goods, charity looks to salvation, loving our neighbors by first loving ourselves: loving with a love that would burn like fire all that stands between God and His creatures. "In the last analysis, charity is to make a gift of God to God by means of the ego and through beings. It communicates a blessing the source of which is God and communicates it to the neighbor who, insofar as he is the object of love, is God's representative."

✢ Chapter 12 ✢

Veracity

To be perfectly objective is to die a little.

$\mathcal{T}$he third of the fundamental virtues is veracity. Like humility and charity, it is related to a distinct stage of the spiritual journey. Where humility corresponds to the first level of purity and purgation, and where charity corresponds to the second level of illumination and expansion, veracity—or objectivity—corresponds to the third, and highest, level of union or perfection. As I pointed out earlier, these stages are not discrete or successive, but are meant to build upon each other like the three dimensions of space. It would obviously be foolish to think that one somehow concludes being humble or stops being pure before advancing to the illumined life of love. On the contrary, love presupposes a continuing awareness of our nothingness before God, and in a similar way both humility and charity are taken up together in the perfection of veracity.

While the first two virtues contribute to the third, they also presuppose it. Humility and love are both rooted in respect for the Truth. It is not only where they are headed, but where they must start, and this fact of course takes us back to the metaphysician's insistence upon the primacy of knowledge. Humility is seeing oneself as another, and treating oneself as severely as the Truth requires, while charity is seeing the neighbor as oneself, and treating him as indulgently as the Truth will allow. Truth is essential in each case. Without Truth, there would simply be no humility and charity at all, and without veracity, Truth would remain inoperative in the soul of the pilgrim. Before undertaking the life of Virtue, we must therefore know at least something of the Truth we seek, and this is why we began our discussion of the journey with a map.

We could make the same point in these terms: *Karma yoga* or the way of works and action, while not of course rejecting either love or veracity, tends to stress ascetic struggle and the virtue of humility. *Bhakti yoga* or the way of devotion, without excluding humility and veracity, stresses love or charity. As for *jnana yoga* or the way of knowledge, it focuses above all on veracity. It in no way dismisses the importance of humility or charity, but at the same time it is based on the fact that Truth must be the foundation for everything else in the spiritual life. If you think of the virtues with regard to their metaphysical meaning or content, these relationships become even clearer. Humility means seeing ourselves in light of the transcendence, exclusiveness, and unicity of the Absolute. Charity means seeing our neighbor in light of the immanence, inclusiveness, and totality of the Infinite. Veracity means seeing everything, ourselves and our neighbors included, in light of that Supreme Reality whose unity is at once transcendent and immanent, exclusive and inclusive, absolute and infinite.

The virtue of veracity can also be called objectivity. This word, however, may need a little explaining. I find that certain unfortunate habits of language have led many people to confuse objectivity with empirical science. An object, to them, means a physical or material thing, and they have been led by the propagandists of a strict materialism to suppose that such things alone are verifiably real, and that those who study them are alone in being truly objective. People who adopt this position are not necessarily materialists themselves. They may well be religious believers, with a faith in God and a hope for immortality. Nevertheless their error in regard to this point represents at least a partial victory of materialism, even as fideism represents a partial victory of rationalism. For they inevitably end up thinking of faith as a private, individual, and subjective affair, to be shared perhaps with other like-minded believers, but incapable of proof or authentication, and thus inappropriate for the public domain. To issue a call for objectivity in anything but the scientific arena of empirical quantity will seem to such people not just a mistake but a kind of indiscretion. In the eyes of the *bhakta* in particular, objectivity sometimes sounds like impiety, for he equates the objective with empirical measurement and calculation, and hence with coldness, insensitivity, and a lack of love, not understanding that "the criterion of objectivity is reality and not the tone or the facial expression; nor above all a sham, inhuman, and insolent placidity."

From the perspective of *gnosis*, however, the identification of Truth with the material order is completely mistaken. There is actually nothing more subjective than a purely quantitative assessment of things, which cannot but stop short at their perceptual surface. After all, the empirical world is but the dream of the ego, both the ego as such and my own particular ego. What I see in the empirical world around me is the outside of my individuality, just as my individual being is the inside of what I see. Far from providing an utterly impartial or objective account of reality, empirical data are but the reflections of reflections. To use a different image, they show us only the tip of the iceberg. To be truly objective is to take account of this metaphysical fact. It is to approach things, not with a view to what the ego wants or prefers, but simply with regard to what is. This is why it is said that "to be perfectly objective is to die a little," for to go beyond what is merely wanted is to go beyond the one who wants, and this is *me*. How am I to do this? What practical steps should be taken? How exactly does veracity express itself in the spiritual life?

Veracity at the very least means telling the Truth—saying of what is that it is—without pretense, distortion, exaggeration, or dissimulation. But Truth concerns much more than just our speech. It refers fundamentally to an entire manner of thinking, breathing, living, being, which accords in all ways with the nature of things. Veracity means conducting our lives in a proportionate and consequential way while consistently taking account of the Truth in little things just as much as in big ones. To be proportionate is to act in keeping with our position in space, and to be consequential is to act with a view to the present moment of time. Punctuality, grammatical precision, and courtesy are all modes of veracity, and on their own plane they are no less important to the spiritual life than doctrinal orthodoxy. Clearly no formula or enumeration of rules could specify all the possibilities in this domain, but perhaps if I mentioned just two of the characteristic signs of this virtue, they could serve to point you forward toward others. Even here, you will notice, there are no hard and fast boundaries, for the two examples are two sides of one coin.

First, there is discipline, and this includes both an internal and an external dimension. "To be disciplined is, intrinsically, to dominate oneself and, extrinsically, to do things correctly." The former has to do with mastering our passions, refusing to allow them to rule our lives. Self-mastery is closely connected with nobility or dignity, which is "the ontological awareness an individual has of his supraindividual reality." Mastery "requires a certain impassibility—thereby manifesting the 'motionless Mover' and the sense of the sacred."

I should explain perhaps that discipline and self-domination do not "exclude the natural impulses of the soul, as is shown by the lives of the sages and saints, and above all by everyday experience." We are to harness our passions and affective impulses, not destroy them, for they are a part of human nature itself. But they are not the whole of that nature, and they need to be put in their place, in subordination to the intelligence, if we mean to honor the Truth. Putting them in their place is possible, however, only for the man who has transcended his ego or individuality. "Transcending oneself: this is the great imperative of the human condition; and there is another that anticipates it and at the same time prolongs it: dominating oneself. The noble man is one who dominates himself; the holy man is one who transcends himself."

As for the external or extrinsic aspect of discipline—that is, correct and consequential action—this means that we must "do nothing by halves or against the logic of things." Whatever is worth doing is worth doing as perfectly as possible, without inadvertence or procrastination, and it follows that the man who is spiritually disciplined is going to be "neither negligent nor disordered, nor, one must add, extravagant. In nature, each thing is entirely what it must be, and each thing is in its rightful place according to the laws of hierarchy, equilibrium, proportions, rhythms; freedom of form and movement is combined with an underlying coordination; so it is that perfection of soul requires that the outward be in conformity with the inward."

Hierarchy, equilibrium, proportions, rhythms. A book could be written on each, but let me single out hierarchy for the moment. Spiritual discipline, we could say, is the putting of hierarchy into practice, whether within our own human microcosm or in our relationships with the world outside us. The degrees of Reality mean that with the two exceptions of Beyond-Being at the top and inanimate matter at the bottom, everything in the universe has both a superior and an inferior, and this fact must be taken into account if we wish to live truly. "Every man rules or determines something which is placed in some way in his keeping, even if it is only his own soul, made up of images and desires." In other words, we are each of us nobles with respect to some commoner. "On the other hand, every man is governed or determined by something which in some way surpasses him, even if it is only his Intellect." We are all of us commoners with respect to some nobility. "Thus each man bears in himself the double obligation of duty in relation to the inferior and of piety in relation to the superior, and this double principle is capable of incalculable applications: it includes even inanimate nature, in the sense that everything can serve us, according to circumstances, either as a celestial principle or as a terrestrial substance."

This brings me to mention a second characteristic of veracity. I am not sure what to call it. Perhaps practicality or realism comes the closest to what I have in mind. The true esoterist is no philosopher with his head in the clouds, nor is metaphysics mere speculation. To be attentive to the nature of things is to distinguish not simply between the Absolute and the relative, but on the plane of the relative between what is necessary and what is not: between the important and the unimportant, the relevant and the irrelevant. In fact, one very easy way to distinguish the spiritual teacher from his counterfeits is that the true master both knows and knows how. Because he sees all things in light of principles, he is of all men the most direct and efficient when it comes to the facts and needs of terrestrial life. For principles apply by their very nature to everything. Rather than distracting me from what has to be done, metaphysics gives me a focus, situating the many things which demand my attention by shedding light on their relative positions in the scale of Reality. It helps me to understand that my primary responsibility before God is to save my soul, and in light of this knowledge, other things begin to fall very naturally into the proper places. All the energy that I wasted before in anxiety over what should be done is now conserved and directed. I see, firstly, that "I am not responsible for what others do; and secondly, I cannot change the world, or do away with every wrong, and I need not fret over this. I am responsible before God for my soul, hence for my spiritual and social duties. I discriminate between what is essential and what is not, or between the Real and the unreal. All else I leave in God's hands."

Veracity means getting on with the business of life, while carefully distinguishing, of course, between business and busyness—between those things that I am truly obliged to do and all the many opportunities for triviality and pettiness with which life is so filled. At the same time, veracity also involves indifference to the fruits of my actions. "Man must do his duty without asking whether he will be victorious or not, for faithfulness to principles has its own intrinsic value; it bears its fruit in itself and means *ipso facto* a victory in the soul of the agent." Similarly the truly practical man is indifferent to the question of whether he has experienced some tangible testimony as to the worth of his deeds. This concern, too, is merely a distraction. If we are acting as we should, then "doubtless, we may feel graces, but we may not base ourselves upon them. God will not ask what we have experienced, but He will ask us what we have done."

Practicality and realism are necessary, but so are discretion and decorum. Or to put it more simply, we need a keen instinct for when enough is enough. From a certain point of view, veracity is just common sense, the sense so often recommended precisely because it is not very common. One must know not only what to do, but how far to go when doing it, and when it would be better not even to start. I am trying to describe in concrete and I hope familiar terms what has otherwise been called a sense of the sacred. For the sacred is more than some arbitrarily defined religious sphere. From the perspective of immanence, all existence is sacred, for Manifestation is of the Principle, and the Principle is present in Manifestation. It follows that even in what may seem a merely "neutral contact with matter—and this is even more true of contact with one's fellow men—man should either not leave any trace or else leave a beneficent trace; he should either enrich or pass unperceived." I realize that the mention of other human beings may make it sound as if we are speaking once again about the first two virtues, humility and charity. You would be right to think this, but only because these virtues are themselves deployments of veracity. And yet where humility and charity are ordinarily thought of in the context of social relationships, or in our relationship with Heaven, veracity extends to our comportment or behavior in general, not only toward other people or God, but toward our entire environment. When the spiritual master refuses to trample on a flower, "it is because the flower is something of God," and because the virtue of veracity calls him to a proportionate action reflecting this Truth. "If a good man had the power utterly to destroy a stone, he would nevertheless not do so without a motive, for the existence of this stone—that quasi-absolute something which distinguishes it from nothingness—is a manifestation of the Principle, and it is therefore sacred." Such discretion or decorum or respect, which is a kind of existential "adequation, parallel to knowledge properly so called," is a "manner of being objective, of being in conformity with reality."

It is time to conclude, but before doing so I need to guard against a possible misunderstanding. Veracity implies discipline, I have said, and this in turn implies that the spiritual life should "allow of no casualness." But at the same time we are to be realistic, and realism among other things implies never forgetting that we live within the play of *Maya*, where the absurd is unavoidable, and where the best weapon against the forces of darkness is often a sense of humor, and a willingness to smile at ourselves. Discipline, proportion, and precision must not tempt us to a sort of perfectionism, leading to strain and bitterness. "If in fact we are saints, that is of interest to Heaven since Heaven is interested in our spiritual welfare; but our individualistic and perfectionistic desire for holiness is of no interest to it. We may pray and ask God to free us from a fault—on condition that we neglect nothing that will help free us from it—but we may not ask God to make us perfect." Undoubtedly "the desire to be perfect is not lacking in logic, but the desire not to be imperfect is more realistic and more concrete, and also more modest." In the final analysis, veracity has to do with striking a balance between dignity and formality, on the one hand, and a childlike spontaneity, on the other.

It all comes back to the playful seriousness that I mentioned when talking about the doctrine of illusion. We have to be serious, for God is absolute, but we must be willing to smile, for He is also infinite.

※ Chapter 13 ※

Predestination and Freedom

Virtue independent of any acceptance of Truth and of any movement towards God is like a crystal with which a man might try to light up a dark place. The crystal is by its nature luminous, but its properties of purity, transparence, and the power to condense luminous rays are inoperative without the presence of light.

*W*ith this we come to the conclusion of our discussion of Virtue and the virtues. Before turning to the next of the essential elements, however, it is important that we spend a few minutes considering a question that often confuses people who are trying to understand man's relationship with God. Like the question of why there is evil, which was discussed under the heading of Truth, this question is unanswerable from the point of view of reason alone. The rationalist is quick to exploit that fact by turning it into an excuse for his skepticism, while for their part religious believers too often excuse their inability to provide an adequate explanation by having recourse to the concept of mystery. There are indeed mysteries, but apart from any effort to situate them in an intelligible framework, they will always seem to the critic to be nothing more than signs of human credulity and lack of rigor.

One might summarize the entire subject of Virtue by saying that knowledge of the Truth obliges us to choose the Truth. Comprehension of God calls for conformation to God. This conformation requires that a man conduct his life in a way that accords with Reality, by eliminating the faults and vices which stand between him and his primordial nature. We are told that "the prerogative of the human state is objectivity, the essential content of which is the Absolute." Objectivity, however, means not only knowledge on the level of the intelligence, but also freedom on the level of the will, and hence a capacity for living the life of Virtue. "Intelligence capable of the Absolute necessarily implies free will." In fact, there is a reciprocal relationship between these elements, for intelligence depends in turn on the will "in the sense that free will can contribute towards actualizing intelligence or on the contrary paralyzing it. It was not without reason that medieval theologians located heresy in the will: intelligence can, in fact, fall into error, but its nature does not allow it to resist Truth indefinitely; for this to happen it needs the intervention of a factor connected with the will."

Truth entails Virtue if we mean to live what we know. Intelligence both implies and depends on free choice. But here is where the question or problem arises. To put it as simply and as starkly as possible: How can I who am nothing choose God who is everything? What sense does will make in the face of the Absolute? This is the classic dilemma of predestination and freedom. How can one account for the sovereignty of God while at the same time preserving human responsibility? Account for and preserve them we must, for both are essential to the moral life and thus to Virtue. Without God, morality collapses for lack of a principle and a proportionate object, and what is God without sovereignty? But without human freedom, moral action would be lacking a responsible agent worthy of praise or blame, reward or punishment, and the possibility of Virtue would again collapse. Neither God nor man may be neglected. And yet it seems to the reason that there is an irreducible opposition between these poles and that one or the other must be discarded. Either God is sovereign, with all things dependent upon His will, and therefore man is not free. Or else man is free to will or to choose for himself, and therefore God is not sovereign. This antinomy results in two extremes: predestinarianism or Divine determinism at one end of the spectrum and atheistic individualism at the other. Either free will is denied for the sake of God, or God is denied for the sake of free will.

As I mentioned already, this problem is similar to the problem of evil. They are alike in their structure, with the Divine Reality placed in competition with something which seems to exclude or to compromise it, and they are thus alike, too, in often serving as excuses for unbelief. For our purposes here, however, the most important resemblance is to be found in their common failure to distinguish between the degrees of Reality. "The question of predestination and the question of evil are the two great problems. But from the standpoint of metaphysical knowledge, the only problem is that of expression through language; the difficulty lies in the fact that the heaviness of language requires almost endless prolixities." I shall do my best not to be prolix, for this part of my book must in fact have an end. But in order to be as succinct as possible, I must rely on your recalling certain points we made earlier in discussing both the levels of the Real and the doctrine of illusion. As always metaphysical teaching is there to remind us of the twofold Truth that while nothing even exists except God, God is at the same time everything which exists—in accordance, once again, with transcendence and immanence. If one sees through this ellipsis into the nature of things, then exposition can be very brief. If one does not, then all the words in the world cannot make up the difference.

To be a man is to be able to choose, for man "is characterized by a free and not merely instinctive will." But to be God is to be sovereign, and this means that "everything that occurs is willed by God," and that "it is impossible for any will to pit itself against the Divine Will." How can both of these propositions be true? The only way to make sense of their apparent contradiction is to return to two of our earlier distinctions: the metaphysical distinction between the Absolute as such and the relative Absolute—between Beyond-Being and Being, or the Divine Essence and the Divine Person—and the no less important distinction, within the microcosm, between the Intellect and the ego. "The situation of man in the face of God evokes the question of knowing which hypostatic mode or ontological degree is involved in this confrontation." We have to remember that in speaking of God, we are referring to the Divine Principle, and that there is a difference within this Principle between the Supreme Reality as such and its self-determination as God the Creator and Sovereign Lord. There is both a "pure Absolute" and a "lesser Absolute." Similarly, it is important to make sure that when speaking of man, we know in any given case whether we are referring to the human individuality or ego or to the supra-individual and transpersonal Intellect. The problem of predestination and freedom comes from confusing these levels—confusing specifically the esoteric and metaphysical relationship between the Supreme Reality and the Intellect with the exoteric and theological relationship between the Divine Person and the human individual.

Strictly speaking, the Divine Essence alone is both truly necessary and truly free. Standing above everything else, at the very summit of the vertical axis which we were envisioning earlier, it alone is so complete, so integral, and so simply itself that necessity is another name for its liberty. As the Absolute, it cannot not be. As the Infinite, it is all possibility. At the opposite end of the spectrum, at the furthest remove from the Divine Essence, where existence trails off into the impossible possibility of nothingness, there is on the contrary complete contingency and complete determination, something that is utterly unnecessary and at the same time utterly without freedom. For below everything else, at the very bottom of the axis of Reality, there is an inversion or parody of Beyond-Being: something so imperfect, so illusory, and so necessitated by conditions outside itself as to be free of any center that could be called its own.

The key to understanding the problem of predestination and freedom is to realize that between these two extremes, at various points along the axis of radiation, everything else is mixed. Nothing is either purely free or completely determined, nor is anything strictly necessary or merely contingent. Things exhibit instead a combination of qualities or attributes in measures proportionate to their places in the scale of Reality. This includes both man and the Divine Person, for both are subject to *Maya* or illusion. To ask, therefore, whether man is free before God is to raise one of those questions "to which the answer is at once 'yes' and 'no.'" We come to yet another case where we must be attentive to different angles of vision. No univocal or unambiguous response is possible—unless, that is, one specifies in precisely which respect, and with regard to what measure, the question is posed. According to the metaphysician, man is predestined in two senses, but man is also free in two senses, with the difference corresponding in each case to the distinction of degrees between the "lesser Absolute," which is Being, and the "pure Absolute," which is Beyond-Being.

Man is predestined, in the first place, in the sense that his choices, real though they are on their level, are always known in advance by the omniscience of the Divine Person. "The idea of predestination is simply an expression, in the language of human ignorance, of the Divine Knowledge that in its perfect simultaneity embraces all possibilities without any restriction." We call this foreknowledge, but it would actually be better called a supraknowledge since God is not in time. He looks instead upon time from a vantage point outside it, whence all its many moments appear as but a single point. "If God is omniscient, He knows future events, or rather events that appear thus to beings limited by time," and "from the moment that He knows them, they appear as predestined relative to the individual." Nevertheless, "the individual will is free insofar as it is real; if it were not in any degree or in any way free it would be deprived of all reality." God's knowledge of what I shall do tomorrow does not deprive me of the freedom to choose what I do. He knows what I shall do before I know it or do it, but only because He sees what I have accomplished, by free choice, before it seems to me that the deed has been done. It is like a man surveying a valley from a mountain peak, who can see where travelers on the road below are headed before they get there. And yet his seeing their movement and their destination does not cause them to move or arrive.

Man is also predestined, on a deeper level, with regard to the Divine Essence. From this point of view, it is not simply that our destinies or goals are envisioned at the level of Being. They are instead the expressions or manifestations of certain possibilities eternally prefigured in the infinitude of Beyond-Being. "The individual will appears in this light as a process that realizes in successive mode the interconnection of the modalities of its initial possibility, which is thus symbolically described or recapitulated." The metaphysical axiom that all things are God from the perspective of immanence means that all of the innumerable choices that I have made and shall yet make in my life are the inevitable working out and summing up of what it is that makes me a unique and irreplaceable creature. But this unique creature is in reality "none other than the substance of a given existential possibility." I am a facet or modality contained from the very beginning in that All-Possibility which is the Infinite. Through his choices and the deeds they give rise to, a man "merely manifests in deferred mode his simultaneous cosmic manifestation; in other words, the individual retraces in an analytic way his synthetic and primordial possibility, which for its part occupies a necessary place in the hierarchy of possibilities, the necessity of each possibility being based metaphysically on the absolute necessity of the Divine All-Possibility." To say anything else would be to think that something could exist outside the scope of the Infinite. But such a pretense of autonomy is as absurd as trying to breathe without air or to swim outside of water. Whatever happens, nothing can surprise the omniscience of the Divine Person. And whatever is, nothing can exceed or escape the illimitable plenitude of the Divine Essence.

This is not to say that man has no liberty, however. Our choices are not in vain. On the contrary, your final destiny still depends very much upon you: upon what you will and what you do—on whether, in short, you live the life of Virtue. So it is crucial that we turn immediately to the senses in which man is free.

We are free, first of all, in the sense that our choices are honored by the will of God at the level of Being. To speak of a will, even the will of God or of Heaven, is to refer to something determinate or set apart from other aspects or faculties—something distinct, for example, from the Divine wisdom, justice, or mercy. But such a determination or distinction does not exist within the Absolute as such, which is perfectly simple. Beyond-Being does not have a will and does not make decisions. Personal attributes like a will pertain instead to the level of Being, which though absolute with respect to existence is relative with respect to the Supreme Reality. Although He is sovereign when compared to His creatures, the Divine Person is nonetheless determined when compared to His Essence. And this determination, which represents a degree of limitation, opens up a certain space in which man can be free: free to seek Him, but also free to turn away. The personal God is not the same as the Infinite or All-Possibility, and this means that there are possibilities as it were outside Him which He is metaphysically obliged to honor. "The very creation of man implies on God's part a certain obligation freely and logically consented to, failing which man would not be man, and God would not be God." It is not for nothing that sacred scriptures speak of rewards and punishments.

If man wishes to be rewarded, then he must choose God, but "man's freedom to choose God is already something of the freedom of God." This observation brings us to a second sense in which we are free. Our freedom to choose the Divine Person comes from our share in the liberty of the Divine Essence. "If we cannot will anything other than what is predestined for us"—and this is true in the two senses already described—"this does not prevent our will being what it is, namely, a relatively real participation in its universal prototype; it is precisely by means of this participation that we feel and live our will as being free."

We are reminded once more of the fact that the human state embraces both divinity and dust. As dust or mere egos, we are virtual nothings in the face of transcendence, and from this point of view, our will is "deprived of all reality"—"or more precisely, it is totally nonexistent." But through that share in divinity which is the Intellect, we are virtual gods in view of immanence, and from this point of view, our "liberty, like all positive qualities, is Divine in itself," just as "a reflection of the sun is identical with the sun, not as a reflection but as light, light being one and indivisible in its essence." What I am is but a possibility that cannot not be, for the necessity of the Divine Essence includes everything possible, and this particular possibility in turn includes by anticipation and in their gradual unfolding each of the many choices I make. In this sense, "the individual 'wants' to be what he 'is.'" But at the same time, the very simplicity of the Essence forbids that its possibilities should be something different from it. It is rather each one of them, and in each it expresses itself in accordance with the appropriate level of Reality. In man, who is able to choose, it includes the choosing. The individual wants to be what he is, and this is one of the senses of predestination. But it could also be said, "more profoundly, that he 'is' what he 'wants': what his possibility, the very one he manifests, wants—or wanted initially," and this of course is one of the senses of freedom. As there is but one who knows, so in the final analysis there is but one who chooses, and this is *Atma* or the Supreme Self, in whom and through whom we have perfect freedom—"on condition that we are liberated from the veils which separate us from our true nature." This condition, as always, is extremely important, for we must never forget that *I* am not *me*. The Self, though everywhere immanent, infinitely transcends the ego.

Let us summarize this difficult topic. Predestination or human determination corresponds, on the one hand, to the omniscience, and thus to the liberty, of the personal God, but it is also a manifestation of the necessity of the Divine Essence. Conversely, free will or human liberty is made possible by the determination, and thus the limitation, of the personal God, but at the same time it is a participation in the freedom of the Divine Essence. Though our choices are known already in Heaven, we are nonetheless free before God, and we are free before Him because we are free within Him—free with the very freedom He is, which is none other than His necessity. "The purpose of freedom is to enable us to choose what we are in the depths of our heart."

Practically speaking, the spiritual journey would not be possible unless in some sense a man was already what he meant to become, and this is the meaning of predestination. The very fact that you have set out on this path makes it clear that God has determined it so, and this I hope will give you confidence. But do not let confidence devolve into presumption, for possibility is not the same as achievement. It is correct to say that "no one escapes his destiny," but "our destiny is dependent on the personal level—high or low—at which we halt, or in which we enclose ourselves." The journey would not be possible were we not in some sense already at the goal. But it would not be necessary unless the goal in another sense still needed reaching, unless we still had to become what we are, and this is the meaning of our freedom. Salvation must be worked out with fear and trembling, even though God is within us to will and to work, and this work is the very essence of Virtue. The fact that you are on the path is no guarantee that you will reach the end, so please be certain to make your choices carefully. To have begun but not to have finished is to exist in a most precarious state, for "when the soul finds itself so to say suspended between two worlds, one already lost and the other not yet reached, only a fundamental virtue together with grace can save it from vertigo, and only this virtue immediately renders it immune to temptations and deviations."

Virtue is something you are. But it is also something you must be.

Beauty

Beauty is the splendor of the True.

—*Plato*

Chapter 14

A Space before God

*Beauty and goodness are the two faces of one and the same
reality, the one outward and the other inward; thus goodness
is internal Beauty, and Beauty is external goodness.*

*W*e come to the third of the indispensable elements in the
spiritual life. I must confess from the start that this will be
the most difficult dimension of *gnosis* to explain. Not that our discussions of Truth and Virtue were easy. You are probably still weigh-
ing what was said on those subjects and perhaps asking yourself
how far you are prepared to go in accepting the propositions and
interpretations of the metaphysician. I do not pretend to have
answered all questions, and there are certainly many blanks that
could still be filled in. And yet there was nothing surprising in these
two elements as such. Any spiritual teacher is going to insist that
Truth and Virtue are necessary to the path, that our journey back
to God is impossible without both doctrine or comprehension and
morality or conformation. No one grows spiritually without discernment or knowledge and without nobility of character.

Beauty, however, will seem less obvious. Its importance is certainly more difficult to get across in words. I am faced at once with
three problems. In the first place, no prose exposition is ever going
to be adequate to the directness and simplicity of Beauty, to its

indisputable but elliptical witness to God. Beauty is essential to the spiritual life precisely because it helps to cut short the verbosity of the discursive mind and to cut through the ego's efforts to weave yet another cloak for itself out of the threads of true doctrine. "Beauty, with its breath of infinity and generosity, breaks down the fixed attitudes and closed systems of this supposedly spiritual egoism." We are therefore faced with a dilemma. We must use the very words which Beauty would have us do without. One wishes to say simply, Look! All the various formulations and considerations which follow are so many ways of encouraging you to see for yourself that Beauty "communicates a substance of Truth, of evidence, and of certitude," and that "it does so in a concrete and existential mode."

There is a second difficulty. For most people today, Beauty is subjective and relative, and they will stoutly resist the suggestion that it might contribute to our reaching something objective and absolute. We have spoken several times about skepticism and relativism with regard to knowledge and morality, and I have briefly described how one might respond to the claim that there is no such thing as Truth, or that Virtue is a matter of personal preference. Unfortunately, there is no analogous argument against the false platitude that Beauty is in the eye of the beholder. This is one reason why those who are objectivists or absolutists with respect to doctrine and morals are often subjectivists when it comes to Beauty. They forget that the true, the good, and the beautiful are together aspects of a single, undivided Reality. If one is prepared to admit the sovereignty and universality of the former two qualities, it is illogical not to do the same in the case of the third.

And yet it is rare indeed even for religious believers to draw this conclusion. This is no doubt partly because their own teachers and spiritual authorities seem in many cases equally oblivious to the essential connection, and this fact presents yet a third obstacle. Those who speak and write about the spiritual life, even persons whose credentials are otherwise beyond dispute, often appear indifferent to the seeker's aesthetic ambience and are sometimes deliberately opposed to the cultivation of Beauty. Either sensible Beauty is considered unimportant, or it is actually denounced as incompatible with our movement toward God. The indifference can be justified to a certain extent by the fact that while Beauty is indeed indispensable for the serious seeker today, it is extrinsic to the search as such. Truth, Virtue, and Prayer are all essential in principle to the spiritual life. No man can do without them whatever the environment or the age in which he lives. Beauty, however, is essential in fact. It has become indispensable for those of us who no longer have the benefit of living in an integral, traditional culture—who are faced at every turn instead with the noise, the ugliness, and the triviality of an increasingly mechanized world. Whatever may have been the case in the past, and whatever might still be true for the exceptional spiritual athlete, it is crucial that the rest of us deliberately seek and actively cultivate a sacred space for our spiritual efforts, and this means at the very least coming to appreciate the importance of Beauty. "In our times, the discerning of forms assumes a quite special importance. Error appears in all the forms which surround us and in which we live," whether in art, music, dress, or architecture. There is a danger with such an environment of its "poisoning our sensibility—even our intellectual sensibility—by introducing into it a kind of false indifference, hardness, and triviality." In such a context, Beauty takes on a very special importance which it did not have for our ancestors. The further removed we become from virgin nature and the daily rhythms of a traditional religious life, the greater the importance of Beauty, "even from the so-called artistic point of view," for aesthetic forms have today become "almost indispensable channels for the actualization of the spiritual deposit of the religion."

As for the outright hostility to Beauty that one sometimes encounters, this undoubtedly stems in part from the fact that "every Beauty is both a closed door and an open door, or in other words, an obstacle and a vehicle: either Beauty separates us from God because it is entirely identified in our mind with its earthly support, which then assumes the role of idol, or Beauty brings us close to God because we perceive in it the vibrations of Beatitude and Infinity, which emanate from Divine Beauty." The ascetical and penitential emphasis of some traditional teachers results from the possibility of idolatry. It guards against the attendant temptation by rejecting all sensible consolations as mere aestheticism. The perspective of *gnosis*, however, is based upon the fact that aesthetic pleasure can nonetheless serve as an opening toward an intuition of Truth and the deepening of Virtue. "An enjoyment which brings man nearer to God is no less profound than suffering, and perhaps in some respects more profound." This is certainly not to deny the legitimacy of asceticism, which can help us to remember concretely that since the Absolute alone is Reality, all else is mere nothingness, let alone a distraction. But we should not go so far as to forget that this same Absolute is also Infinite. With respect to its immanence, whatever exists is in some fashion Divine, including even the simplest of our pleasures and joys. "No doubt, every amusement is a pleasure, but it does not follow that every pleasure is an amusement; otherwise every marriage would be something frivolous, including the wedding at Cana." If we wish to avoid the "icy egoism" that may result from too one-sided a "concern for spiritual love and for mortification," then it is necessary to have "the sense of the Divine perfume in the natural pleasures that life here below offers us." Of course it is essential that we "partake of them with nobleness" and hence with detachment. Nobility is a "consciousness of God," which "on the one hand annuls, in a certain fashion, both forms and qualities, and on the other confers on them a value that transcends them." Detachment means that while "the soul is so to say impregnated with death," it remains by compensation "aware of the indestructibility of earthly beauties; for Beauty cannot be destroyed; it withdraws into its archetypes and into its essence, where it is reborn, immortal, in the blessed nearness of God."

It might be helpful to return to our image of the spiritual life as a journey. Truth, I have said, is at once our starting point and our goal. Without the Truth in the form of a theory or map, we could never begin, and without Truth as a living Reality, we would never come to an end. Prayer is the motive force behind our progress toward this end. It is the name for all that brings us into unity with God. As for Virtue and Beauty, these elements together constitute the space or context where progress toward the goal may occur. Since man has both a soul and a body, this context includes both an internal and an external dimension. Virtue corresponds to the former and Beauty to the latter, without there being any hard and fast division between the two.

Virtue is the inward space of the soul in which the journey takes place, while Beauty is the outward or corporal space. We move in the first and through the second. "In Beauty man 'realizes' in a passive way—as to its perception—and outwardly—as to its production—that which he should himself 'be' in an active and inward fashion." This is why we can say that "Virtue is Beauty of the soul, as Beauty is the Virtue of forms," and why "if the fundamental virtues are beauties, conversely each sensible beauty bears witness to the virtues." A given sensible or external beauty can be said to be "'humble' because it submits to the universal laws and, because of this, excludes all excess." At the same time, it is "'charitable' in the sense that it radiates and enriches without ever asking for anything in return." It can be called "pious" or truthful—"that is 'ascendant' or 'essentializing'— because it manifests celestial archetypes." Hence "by loving sensible Beauty intelligently and piously—and thus in a contemplative manner—the soul remembers its own immortal essence." Beauty brings me face to face with my primordial nature, and it calls me to become what I am. "To give oneself to God is the response proportionate to the earthly Beauty in which God, in revealing mercy, has given Himself to man."

This reciprocity between Beauty and Virtue would not exist, however, unless both of them were rooted in and directed toward Truth. As always, the metaphysician wishes to emphasize the primacy of knowledge in our relationship with God. Truth alone keeps Virtue from becoming a matter of individual choices, and it is Truth alone which keeps Beauty from being reduced to an "inexcusable pleasure," or at best to an "expression of piety." It is no accident that those who would define Virtue in terms of what we do or how we act are very often the "partisans of a touchy asceticism," mistrustful of Beauty. For the esoterist, however, who is guided by the nature of things, "perceived Beauty is not only the messenger of a celestial and Divine archetype; it is also, for that very reason, the outward projection of a universal quality immanent in us, and quite obviously more real than our empirical and imperfect ego, gropingly seeking its identity." Where Virtue is fundamentally a question of being, and not just of doing, so Beauty is a question of seeing, and not just of liking or wanting. It is an outward reflection of "that inward release, that detachment, that sort of gentle grandeur that is proper to contemplation, and so to wisdom and to Truth."

To understand what all of this means, we need to go slowly. First, we shall examine the close connection between Beauty and the world as theophany, between aesthetics and traditional cosmology. This will be our task in the next meditation. Once that foundation is established, we can proceed to consider the Beauty of the human body, the role of sacred art in the spiritual life, and finally some practical implications of Beauty for how we live our daily lives.

Chapter 15

The World as Symbol

Things are in God and God is in things with a kind of discontinuous continuity.

"*E*soterically speaking, there are only two relationships to take into consideration, that of transcendence and that of immanence: according to the first, the reality of Substance annihilates that of the accident; according to the second, the qualities of the accident—starting with their reality—cannot but be those of Substance."

On the one hand, insofar as it cannot not be, the Supreme Reality is utterly different from anything else. It is independent, transcendent, and absolute, and compared to it, no other thing can be truly said to exist. The world and everything in it is nothing, and all that we see around us is false. But on the other hand, insofar as it is without any limits, the Supreme Reality is intimately connected with everything else, or rather everything is connected with it. It is infinite, immanent, and everywhere present, and for this reason, whatever exists is in some fashion it. The world and everything in it is God, and all that we see around us is true. In short, God is all-exclusive by virtue of His unicity or uniqueness. But at the same time, He is all-inclusive by virtue of His totality and plenitude.

105

I told you at the start, in the Introduction to these meditations, that these two principial truths would be the basis for our treatment of virtually everything else, and you have since been provided with several examples of their manifold applications. Transcendence and immanence have been the key to our discussions of the Intellect, the human state, the degrees of Reality, the meaning of sin, and the relationship between free will and predestination. Indeed, if God were not at once both without and within—beyond ourselves and the world, and yet equally at their center—there would be no such thing as the spiritual journey in the first place. It would be either impossible or unnecessary.

We return to this twofold doctrine here because it provides the framework that is needed if we wish to understand the role of Beauty in the spiritual life. I have explained that Beauty constitutes the space of our movement toward God, specifically the outward or external space which complements the inward space of Virtue. As such a space, Beauty serves to clear away what would otherwise stand in the way of our reaching the transcendent Truth, and it corresponds from this point of view to the Divine absoluteness. By displacing all disproportion and ugliness, Beauty performs what the theologians would call an apophatic role. It negates everything that is not in keeping with God. The resulting openness is no nullity or vacuum, however. It is filled to the very brim with the vibrant presence and proximity of the Divine infinitude, and as such a fullness, Beauty brings us into immediate contact with the immanent Truth which it is. From this point of view, the role of Beauty is cataphatic or affirmative as it works by analogy and not opposition. "Beauty is in one sense always more than it gives, but in another sense it always gives more than it is. In the first sense, the Essence shows itself as appearance; in the second, the appearance communicates the Essence." The former is the result of transcendence and the latter of immanence. But there is also a measure of immanence within the transcendence and a measure of transcendence within the immanence. Beauty always points to a Reality beyond itself even in the very act of allowing what is beyond to be felt as within, and this takes us back to the metaphysical fact that there is not only the Principle and Manifestation, but Manifestation within the Principle. On the other hand, Beauty brings us into contact with nothing short of Reality even while reminding us that the Real is beyond, and this is because there is not only Manifestation within the Principle, but the Principle within Manifestation.

This background in the doctrine of the degrees of Reality is essential when it comes to countering the claim, which I mentioned in our last discussion, that Beauty is a matter of opinion alone—that it is merely subjective. I have already admitted that there is no way of proving that this claim is wrong. Those who suppose that personal taste or individual preference can account for all matters aesthetic are not going to be converted by argument. If they wish to think that when I call something beautiful, I am simply projecting my internal feelings upon a neutral object, then there is nothing I can do for them by logic alone. A change of heart will come about not by listening to proofs, but by practical experience. If you find yourself dubious, all I can do is ask that you make an experiment. Like the scientist who wishes to verify a hypothesis, you will have to test what the perennial philosophers say in the laboratory of your own life. And this will mean following up on certain concrete suggestions that I shall be making below. For now I simply wish to elaborate the theory itself, to situate the significance of Beauty in relationship to the metaphysical and cosmological principles which give it its objectivity and thus its spiritual power.

Reality comprises various levels or planes, and this fact has important implications for fully grasping the meaning of Beauty. "There is not only this hierarchy" of levels, however. "There is also in the Universe the diversifying manifestation of the positive possibilities included in the Divine Potentiality." This means that to the metaphysical doctrine of degrees, by virtue of which "the ugly is less real than the beautiful," we shall have to add now as a cosmological corollary that Reality is also a matter of dimensions or modes, and that on each level in the universal hierarchy, one can find echoes or reflections of all of God's attributes. This, too, is closely connected to the spiritual function of Beauty. Let me try to explain.

God is both absolute and infinite. As the Infinite, He is the continuous source of all things—not simply their chronological origin, but their ontological foundation during the entire term of their existence. Thus all things are manifestations of God. They show Him forth in two ways: first, by the very fact that they are something and not nothing, and second, in their specific qualities, functions, and relationships, which are what they are because God is within them. We considered this point earlier in connection with the proofs of God. "Whatever be the object envisaged, there springs from its existential

center an ontological ray," a line of connection between its existence
and Being, "whereby the object in question is attached, through its
subtle or animic root, to its luminous and celestial prototype," to its
corresponding idea in the mind of God. But the Divine ideas are
themselves multiple expressions, at the level of Being or the Divine
Person, of the simplicity and indeterminacy of the Supreme Reality,
where "every quality is every other" in "non-distinction." It follows
from this that "in principle it is possible for us to attain the heavenly
Essence by taking anything whatever as starting point." With the
possibility of this attainment in mind, we can define Beauty by saying that it is the name for the point of intersection between a given
phenomenon and the "ontological ray" which connects the summit of
Reality to the very edge of nothingness and which passes through all
the beings between. The perception of Beauty is an invitation to proceed through that phenomenon into its celestial model, and thence
into its supra-ontological Source.

Within Beauty in the singular, there are beauties in the plural, for
things are diverse, and here is where the question of modes arises.
The beauty of one creature is not that of another. On the plane of
manifestation, the infinity of God is expressed in a multiplicity of
perfections, each leading us back toward a distinct but undivided
aspect or attribute of the Divine Substance. The contemplative study
of these perfections is the basis for the cosmological sciences, which
were traditionally integrated into the spiritual path as the modes
became openings to Truth, complements of Virtue, and supports for
Prayer. A sensitivity to the objective beauty of things is the basis for
astrology, geomancy, alchemy, numerology, physiognomy, and other
traditional sciences, which unlike their strictly empirical successors
were always directed to a spiritual end—not to prediction, control, or
mere description on the material or natural plane alone.

In order for this way of looking at the world to make sense, one
must learn to approach things as symbols rather than as facts or
even signs. Creatures are not simply material objects, nor are they
merely occasions for the horizontal conventions of human language.
They are actual participants through their intrinsic qualities in the
vertical realities which they communicate. A dove, for example, is
not just a biological organism, nor does it serve only to provide the
poet with a metaphor of peace. It is itself peace in the form of an animal—whether a given man is a poet or not and whatever the scientist might say about its chemical composition. "Divine manifesta-

tion, around us and in us, prolongs and projects the Principle and is identified with it precisely in respect of the immanent Divine quality; the sun is really the Principle perceived through existential veils; water is really universal Passivity perceived through the same veils." Please understand that I am not just describing how the world happens to appear to human perception. If you wish to understand traditional cosmology, and hence the true significance of Beauty, you must come to grips with the fact that a creature is what it is, with all of its distinguishing properties, precisely because of its own intrinsic level of discernment. The capacities, the mobility, the very shape and color and texture of a creature—in short, its Beauty—are the outside of its awareness of Truth. "If gold is not lead, that is because it 'knows' the Divine better. Its 'knowledge' is in its very form, and this amounts to saying that it does not belong to it in its own right, since matter cannot know. Nonetheless we can say that the rose differs from the water lily by its intellectual particularity, by its 'way of knowing,' and so by its mode of intelligence. Beings possess intelligence in their form to the extent that they are 'peripheral' or 'passive' and in their essence to the extent that they are 'central,' 'active,' and 'conscious.' A noble animal or a lovely flower is 'intellectually' superior to a base man. God reveals himself to the plant in the form of the light of the sun. The plant irresistibly turns itself towards the light; it could not be atheistical or impious."

I realize that this may prove rather hard to digest. It is a radically different way of looking at the world from what most of us are familiar with. Modern science has taught us to use only our reason while neglecting the Intellect, to limit our knowledge to the data provided by our physical senses to the exclusion of inspiration and Revelation, and to concentrate almost solely on the material composition and efficient causes of things. We are encouraged to ask what things are made of and how they work, but not what they mean or why they were made. The result is that many people seem to have lost a sense of the sacred, an intuitive awareness of the world as symbol and theophany. They take "matter as their starting point, as if it were a primordial and stable fact, whereas it is only a movement, a sort of transitory contraction of a substance that is in itself inaccessible to our senses," and in doing so, they have exchanged the knowledge which "consists in seeing nothing but God," or "God in all things," or even "things 'and' God," for the "ignorance that sees only things and excludes God." They have become blind to "the qualitative and quasi-absolute element which is present at the center and in the arteries of the cosmos, and which flashes forth to produce the phenomenon of the sacred." And they have forgotten that "what matters is not to know that the earth turns round the sun, or to grasp the molecular structure of matter, but to discern the cosmic value—orientated towards the absolute Cause—of the phenomena which surround us, and according to the way that they surround us." In a word, they have lost touch with Beauty.

Doing justice to the richness and subtlety of the traditional cosmological vision is obviously out of the question in the present context. An adequate exposition of the symbolic sciences would require a separate book of its own. I would, however, like to give you just a taste of the Beauty which opens up to this vision, and I can perhaps do this best with a brief numerological look at the world.

It is a basic principle of all traditional cosmologies that numbers have qualitative properties. More than mere signs of quantity, numbers have distinctive qualities corresponding to fundamental forms and forces in the universe around us as well as to certain aspects of the human soul. "While one obtains ordinary numbers by addition, qualitative number results on the contrary from an internal or intrinsic differentiation of principial unity; it is not added to anything and does not depart from unity." The numbers are so many forms or expressions of oneness. This can be glimpsed in geometrical figures, where different numbers of sides together constitute different shapes, each with its own unique quality. For example, "the triangle is harmony," and "the square, stability." Traditionally, the specific quality or meaning of a given number will vary depending upon whether it is envisioned as applying vertically to the levels of Reality or horizontally to the modes of a single level. If we limit our attention for now to the numbers one through four, certain of their meanings might be suggested as follows.

Horizontal unity means that God alone is real, while vertical unity, through which the Divine unicity is projected onto the plane of existence, reminds us that whatever is, is God. Horizontal duality, on the other hand, corresponds to the distinction in God between the Absolute and the Infinite. Vertical duality, accounting for the descent of the Principle into Manifestation, gives rise in the world to the difference between "the rigorous and the gentle, the active and the passive, the contractive and the expansive." Herein lies the meaning of the Taoist *yin* and *yang*. Horizontal trinity pertains within God to what the Hindus call *Satchitananda*—to the Divine modes of Being,

Consciousness, and Beatitude, or to Power, Wisdom, and Goodness. At the same time, because of the vertical deployment of the number three as Beyond-Being, Being, and Existence, the horizontal trinity within the Principle is projected into the world or macrocosm, and one result is the three *gunas* of Hindu cosmology: *sattwa* or the ascending quality of things, *rajas* or the expansive quality or tendency, and *tamas*, which is the descending tendency. The Divine trinity is also reflected in man the microcosm, above all in his faculties of will, intelligence, and sentiment. Finally, horizontal quaternity is the intrinsic relation in God among the Divine attributes of Purity, Life, Strength, and Peace. Vertically, the number four corresponds to the Principle, Manifestation in the Principle, the Principle in Manifestation, and Manifestation as such. On the last of these levels, quaternity makes itself known in the macrocosm as the four cardinal points—North, South, East, and West—and in the four primary qualities of cold, heat, dryness, and moisture, while in the human microcosm it can be seen as "the quaternity of the spiritual or moral principles": namely, "detachment, generosity, vigilance, gratitude."

This sketch of course provides only the barest of hints and no more, provocations toward seeing the universe from just one of several possible symbolic angles. It is far less important for our purposes here than the fundamental metaphysical and cosmological principles which it is designed to illustrate. The essential point to be grasped is that the unicity of the Supreme Reality is constantly being expressed both around us and in us in the totality of creation. All of "nature is like a moving veil before an immutable supernature," and to see it as such, to be aware of the "metaphysical transparency of phenomena," is to be in touch with the essential meaning of Beauty. It is to have a sense of the sacred, of the revelatory "interference of the uncreated in the created, of the eternal in time, of the infinite in space, of the supra-formal in forms." Like the sacred, Beauty is "the mysterious introduction into one realm of existence of a presence which in reality contains and transcends that realm and could cause it to burst asunder in a sort of Divine explosion," but which nonetheless by the merciful gift of its life condescends to sustain and to glorify even the most fragile of creatures.

Beauty is what we experience when we are aware of this transcendence and condescension combined. It is invincible gentleness and inviolable mercy. It is the radiation of the high in the low, tempered to the weakness of man, but filled with the power of God.

Chapter 16

The Message of the Human Body

*The body invites to adoration by its very theomorphic form,
and that is why it can be the vehicle of a celestial presence
that in principle is salvific.*

I warned you when we first began talking about Beauty that it
would be very difficult to get my point across in words. Expository prose is by definition abstract, and I suspect that the last two
meditations will have seemed rarified indeed. This presents a problem. Abstractions are just what we do not want at the moment.
Beauty is of importance to the spiritual life precisely because it
helps to keep us from being too abstract. It is there to protect us
from getting lost in ideas. Beauty serves to remind us that God is
not only transcendent, beyond even the loftiest thoughts we might
think, but also immanent, and thus immediately present even in the
very least of all material forms.

Up to this point, my exposition of the perennial philosophy has
been guided in large part by the idea of hierarchy, symbolized by a
vertical axis. From this point of view, Reality may be said to increase
as one moves away from the physical world. Matter represents the
extreme limit of Manifestation, the lowest rung of the ontological
ladder, situated at the greatest distance from Beyond-Being. It is
crucial, however, that this hierarchical picture, with God at the very

113

top of the universe, not be allowed to eclipse the equally valid image of concentric spheres, with its equally important recognition that God is also at the very center of things. In our deference to the Divine transcendence, we must not lose touch with the Divine immanence. The Supreme Reality is not only far above but deep within the world, and the physical universe is simply its most exterior shell.

In order to assist in holding this paradox together, I must introduce a doctrine which has not yet been mentioned. Our teachers call it the law of inverse analogy. It is "the metaphysical law in virtue of which the analogy between the principial and manifested orders is reversed, in the sense that what is principially great will be small in the manifested order and that which is inward in the Principle will appear as outward in Manifestation." Consider a tree standing near a pool of water, and picture the reflection of the tree on the surface of the water. You know, of course, that a reversal or inversion takes place, and that the bottom of the actual tree will appear at the top of the reflection, while the top of the tree will be mirrored at the bottom of its image. We are told that a similar reversal takes place in the relationship between the Principle and Manifestation. The latter is the mirror of the former, and as with all mirrors, the order in which things appear is just the opposite of what they really are. "In consequence of this analogy, the highest realities are most clearly manifested in their remotest reflections, namely, in the sensible or material order, and herein lies the deepest meaning of the proverb 'Extremes meet.'" Think back to our discussion of *Maya* or illusion. There are not only degrees or levels of Reality. We must also take account of a certain fluidity or flexibility among the levels, which allows for changes of position within the hierarchy depending upon one's angle of vision. The law of inverse analogy is closely connected to these changes, and it helps to remind us that in Reality, unicity and totality are together joined in unity.

It follows from this law that the very solidity and facticity of physical objects, together with their shapes and sounds, their colors and textures, can provide us with a more powerful and in a sense more adequate expression of God than all the conceptual formulations in the world, caught as the latter are in the middle, between the extremes of pure spirit and matter. Here is where Beauty and the sense of the sacred come in. We discussed in the last section how all things can be seen as participants in the celestial qualities to which they point. Beauty was described as the name for that pointing. But lest you suppose that Beauty merely points away from the things themselves, it is important to stress the word *participants*. It is in being what and how they are, and not because of what they are not, that physical objects show forth the Divine. "Sensible forms correspond with exactness to intellections." Their visible and tangible Beauty provides in fact a more immediate witness to God than the interior goodness of the virtuous soul. This is because "the Beauty of God corresponds to a deeper reality than His Goodness"—owing once again to inverse analogy, and "no matter how paradoxical this may appear at first sight." What God really is in His Essence is Beauty— "God is beautiful, and He loves beauty"—while righteousness, mercy, compassion, and justice pertain instead to the relatively absolute level of the Divine Person.

But all of this talk is still much too abstract and vague. In order to provide some focus and to stimulate if I can a concrete realization of what we are talking about, I would like to spend the rest of this chapter concentrating on one sensible form in particular: the human body. Since "there is nothing in the macrocosm that does not derive from the metacosm and which is not to be found again in the microcosm," we may expect to find that the law of inverse analogy is also at work in ourselves.

Man's body, like everything else in the physical universe, is a visible manifestation of the invisible Principle. In the perspective of *gnosis*, he was not originally "a simian being barely capable of speaking and standing upright; he was a quasi-immaterial being enclosed in an aura still celestial, but deposited on earth, an aura similar to the 'chariot of fire' of Elijah or the 'cloud' that enveloped Christ's ascension." Beyond-Being determines itself as Being, and Being is expressed as Existence. So also in the microcosm, the Intellect or spiritual dimension of man is the source of his soul and body. This is the very reverse of the modern evolutionary view, which supposes that "matter is the 'alpha' which gave to everything its beginning"— that "the origin of our ego, our intelligence, and our thoughts is in our bones, our muscles, our organs." For the metaphysician, our bones and other physical elements are instead the coagulations or condensations of incorporeal energies, themselves the subtle expression of celestial archetypes.

This is not to demean or belittle the physical order, however. As I explained at the outset of our discussion of Truth, *gnosis* is not gnosticism. Matter comes last in the cosmogonic sequence, but this does not mean that it is cut off from God, or that our bodies are somehow opposed to God—and therefore to be opposed for God's sake. On the contrary, to say that man is made in the image of God is to speak a truth about the whole human being. The human microcosm, in all its aspects, is a manifestation of the Divine. In fact, it is the central and most definitive manifestation of God in our world, compared to which all other creatures are peripheral and fragmentary. This centrality pertains just as much to our corporal form as it does to our soul or spirit. "The human body in itself is a symbol-sacrament because it is 'made in the image of God.'" The soul is not the image to the exclusion of the body, nor is the body on the other hand to be honored "to the exclusion of the soul that dwells in it, but together with this soul, for the human body has its form only in virtue of the content for which it is made." This last is a point too often neglected by those who try to reconcile biological evolutionism with their faith in a Divine Creator. They seem to think that our bodies could have arisen just anyhow as long as God was standing ready to insert a human soul at some appropriate later stage. This, however, is the real gnosticism. It assumes that the body has a different source from the rest of our being, and that the dimensions of man are like mechanical parts, bolted together from the outside in. But this is just the reverse of the Truth. While the body is the final dimension of man to be expressed, it is no less an expression than the dimensions preceding it. In fact, given the mirrorlike inversion which characterizes the manifested order, the body can in a certain sense tell us more about God than can our soul. The body is farther from God than the other aspects of man, but it is nevertheless more like Him than anything else in the microcosm. And since man alone is God's true image on earth, it follows that the human body is more like the Divine Reality than anything else in the entire creation. As we reflect therefore upon the importance of Beauty, it is essential that we consider our bodies. What man's Intellect is to the Truth, and what his soul is to Virtue, so is his body to Beauty.

The theomorphic, and therefore theophanic or revelatory, nature of the body can be approached from several points of view. It can be seen, for example, in man's gait and posture, in the distinction between the various regions and parts of the body, and in the complementarity between the masculine and feminine forms. I realize that what I am about to say is going to sound to the cynic contrived, artificial, and merely romantic. After all, such a person "has every interest in making us believe that physical animality is what we are," and he therefore tries to convince us that "it is nature which by its impurities mocks man." What he fails to understand is that just the other way round, "it is man who by his prejudices mocks nature." Nature herself is pure message or symbol. But modern man is too proud to see it as such. To make matters worse, he has the temerity to complain that the world is meaningless. I have already done all I can to persuade those who doubt to try looking anew. To return to those earlier arguments would simply mean more theory, and it is time, I have said, to be concrete. So let me instead simply put forward a few observations. Think of them as photographs of different aspects of the human body, offered more or less without commentary and certainly without demonstration or proof, but with the encouragement that you begin looking for yourself as far as you can without the cynic's prejudice. What exactly is the body showing us?

First, we may take note of our posture and how we move through the world. These are the most obvious expressions of man's deiformity. "What above all distinguishes the human form from animal forms is its direct reference to absoluteness, indicated by its vertical posture." Our verticality "marks not only the summit of earthly creatures, but also—and for that very reason—the exit from their condition." We are a combination essentially of "'verticality' and 'inwardness,' as is attested by those two distinctive characteristics of man which are vertical posture and language." On the one hand, we are transcendence, and on the other, we are immanence. As for man's gait, this is "as evocative as his vertical posture; whereas the animal is horizontal and only advances towards itself—that is, it is enclosed within its own form—man, in advancing, transcends himself; even his forward movement seems vertical; it denotes a pilgrimage towards his Archetype, towards the celestial Kingdom, towards God." One might object that among the primates it is possible to find animals which can stand upright and move in more or less the same ways as a man. But in fact close inspection reveals a world of difference. "Far from being able to be a virtual form of man, the ape incarnates an animal desire to be human, hence a desire of imitation and usurpation; but it finds itself as if before a closed door and falls back all the more heavily into its animality, the perfect innocence of which it can no longer capture." Its likeness to man is no more than a parody.

Second, the regions of man's body. "As every form has a cause and a meaning, all the parts of the body are to some degree or other expressions of our being." We may look, in the first place, at the front and back of the body. "The beauty of the anterior side of the human body indicates the nobleness on the one hand of man's vocational end, and on the other hand of his manner of approaching it; it indicates that man directs himself toward God and that he does so in a manner that is 'humanly Divine.'" The back also has its meaning. "It indicates on the one hand the noble innocence of the origin, and on the other hand the noble manner of leaving behind himself what has been transcended; it expresses, positively, whence we have come and, negatively, how we turn our backs to what is no longer ourselves. Man comes from God, and he goes towards God; but at the same time, he draws away from an imperfection which is no longer his own and draws nearer to a perfection which is not yet his. His 'becoming' bears the imprint of a 'being'; he is that which he becomes, and he becomes that which he is." It is helpful to take note of other distinctions as well. "Looking at man from the outside, two formal elements can be distinguished, the body and the head, and it can be said that each alike manifests a third element which is hidden, namely the heart. The outer man is perfect to the extent that his face and body express the heart, not only by Beauty, but also, and indeed above all, by interiorization," by prayer and contemplativity. As for the face, three parts may be distinguished: "the forehead along with the eyes, then the nose, and then the mouth along with the chin; these elements correspond respectively to the intellective nature, the sensitive or 'instinctive' nature, and the volitive nature." The face is a visible text of the soul—a symbol of our thinking, our feeling, and our willing.

Yet another angle of approach permits us to see that the body as a whole includes three fundamental regions: "the body properly socalled, the head, and the sexual parts; these are almost three different subjectivities." Looking at our physical form in this way, we can observe that "the face expresses a thought, a becoming aware of something, a truth; the body, for its part, expresses a being, an existential synthesis; and the sexual parts, a love both creative and liberating: mystery of the generous substance that unfolds in the accidents, and of the blessed accidents that flow back towards the substance; glory of self-giving, and glory of delivering. The human body in its integrality is intelligence, existence, love; certitude, serenity, and faith."

The mention of sexuality leads, thirdly, to the complementarity between the male and female bodies, which is itself a revelation of the God in whose image both are made. "As symbols, the masculine body indicates a victory of the Spirit over chaos, and the feminine body, a deliverance of form by Essence; the first is like a magic sign which would subjugate the blind forces of the Universe, and the second like celestial music which would give back to fallen matter its paradisiac transparency, or which, to use the language of Taoism, would make trees flower beneath the snow." Once again we are brought back to the Absolute and the Infinite, to transcendence and immanence. "The masculine body accentuates the first aspect, and the feminine body, the second." Each "manifests modes of perfection by definition evoked by its respective sex; all cosmic qualities are divided in fact into two complementary groups: the rigorous and the gentle, the active and the passive, the contractive and the expansive." These are the *yang* and the *yin* of the Far Eastern tradition, which I mentioned in the last meditation, expressed on the human plane as the male and the female. "*A priori*, virility refers to the Principle, and femininity to Manifestation; but in an altogether different respect, that of complementarity *in divinis*, the masculine body expresses Transcendence, and the feminine body, Immanence." Man "brings the chaos of existence back to order, that is he brings blind substance back to its ontological meaning and thus constitutes a reference point between Earth and Heaven, a 'sign-post' pointing towards God." Woman, on the other hand, "brings the segmentation of form back to unitive life, reducing form, which is a death, to Essence—at least symbolically and virtually—so that it vibrates with a joy which is at the same time a nostalgia for the Infinite." The masculine body is generous overflowing, and the feminine body is innocent receptivity.

This metaphysical meaning of our bodies is at the root of the erotic love between man and woman. "As a sexual being, woman seeks her center in man," while man for his part "seeks his vital space" in woman. "Man stabilizes woman, woman vivifies man." In his "lunar and receptive aspect," man "'withers away' without the woman-sun that infuses into the virile genius what it needs in order to blossom; inversely, man-sun confers on woman the light that permits her to realize her identity by prolonging the function of the sun." We are speaking in part of the many modes of relationship which can exist between the sexes, including the sexual act itself, but at the same time all these meanings are signified in advance by the respective forms themselves. "Man expresses knowledge and woman, love. Also, the masculine body is more 'geometrical'—it is in a way the 'abstract' image of the Divine Person—while the feminine body is 'musical' and appears as a 'concrete' expression of our existential Substance and, *in divinis*, of the infinite Beatitude. The feminine body is compounded of nobility and innocence." Its nobility is manifested by "its vertical lines, and its innocent fecundity by its curves." Thus, "the beauty of woman appears to man as the revelation of the blissful Essence of which he is himself as it were a crystallization."

This is enough to provoke further reflection. It is time to bring this meditation to a close. The conclusion takes the form of a caution. In my experience, a person either sees what we have been talking about, or else he does not. He is able to discern Truth in the Beauty of the human body, or else all this strikes him as the merest fancy. Arguments will be without avail. If you are someone who does see— if these observations have struck you as accurate, or if they have at least led you to attend more carefully to a region of experience that was before neglected—then you may well rejoice in this most immediate and proximate of revelations. Your very substance, to say nothing of its proportionate carriage and bearing, can become for you a perpetual reminder of God. Touch, posture, movement, breath—an inward sense of one's dynamic solidity—these can be the space for your Prayer: provided, of course, that you always keep in mind that God, while within, is beyond. Never forget that though the body is everything, it is equally nothing. Reverence and detachment are both required.

On the other hand, you may be a person who finds these observations unsettling or distracting, or perhaps just silly. I mentioned the cynic a few pages ago, but I am not in this case talking about sarcasm or ridicule. I rather doubt that a cynic would have come quite so far in this book in the first place. You may however be someone who finds all this talk about man's physical form to be nothing but an invitation to passion. Have we not been warned against the temptations of the flesh? If this is your response, I would simply point out that "the profanation of human Beauty by the passions in no way authorizes contempt for this work of the Creator." There are of course such things as unchastity, perversion, and subhuman behavior, and we have unfortunately seen much of them in our day. But like all the other sins, sexual immorality is a powerful testimony to the intrinsic goodness of what it twists and distorts. In the perspective of *gnosis*, human sexuality, like all things in man, is a pointer toward God, and its misuse as a means of merely physical pleasure is simply a case of corruption, of the best becoming the worst.

But my aim has not been to speak about human behavior, whether moral or not. The essential point of this chapter was to insist that "the theophanic quality of the human body resides uniquely in its form, and not in the sanctity of the soul inhabiting it," nor therefore in the degree of Virtue involved in its actions. The metaphysician certainly does not wish to condone unchastity or its attendant vices. But he does mean to underscore an important principle too often overlooked by the moralist: "outward Beauty, even when combined with an inner ugliness, testifies to Beauty as such, which is of a celestial nature and must not be scorned in any of its manifestations. The calumny of physical beauty by many ascetics can be useful in regard to human weakness, but it is nonetheless inadequate and impious from a more profound point of view."

The body may be considered a revelation of God. It is not necessary however that everyone should see it as such, not even everyone following the path of knowledge. If you do not, my advice is to go on to something else and not to think any further about it. The body as Beauty can be a very powerful support for one's Prayer, but it is certainly not obligatory that it should be, and no amount of cogitation is going to make it so. I end with what has become a recurrent theme: you must simply look. Not to thinking but to seeing does Beauty make itself known.

⚜ Chapter 17 ⚜

Sacred Art

This is the mission of art: to remove the shells in order to reveal the kernels; to distill the materials until the essences are extracted. Nobility is nothing else but a natural disposition for this alchemy, and this on all planes.

I began our meditations on Beauty with a few words about its relationship to Virtue. We saw that together they constitute a space or an opening for the practice of Prayer in response to the Truth. Next I encouraged you to begin trying to see the world as symbol by describing the cosmological and theophanic significance of Beauty. Like everything else in the way of knowledge, Beauty is to be understood in connection with the nature of things. Far from a luxury, it is the objective point of conjunction between visible creatures and their invisible Source. In order to make this teaching more immediate and concrete, we then spent some time in the last chapter talking about the human body as an especially striking example of the message which Beauty brings us from God.

When discussing Beauty, however, one must at some point say a few things, not just about spirituality, cosmology, and the human form, but about the nature and purpose of sacred art. Much could be said on this topic. My intentions here are quite modest. I simply wish to underscore the great importance of art for the serious seeker. The perennial philosophers take art very seriously, and I would encourage you to make the experiment of taking it seriously yourself. If you do, you will discover that the artistic forms with which we surround ourselves can have enormous consequences in the spiritual life. "Nothing can be better fitted to influence the deeper dispositions of the soul than sacred art," which "conveys transcendent values and communicates an intelligence." Such art has a "supernatural value" because it is "the form of what lies beyond form; it is the image of the Uncreated, the language of Silence." Sacred art can thus assist in focusing our attention and directing it toward God, for in keeping with the Absolute and the Infinite, "there is in the sacred an aspect of rigor, invincibility, and inviolability, and an aspect of gentleness, appeasement, and mercy; a mode of immobilizing fascination and a mode of liberating attraction." On the other hand, nothing can be more dangerous and distracting for the soul, "nothing is able to offer irreligion a more immediately tangible nourishment," than an art which "takes into consideration sentimentality only," or which believes that "there are relativities which bear their adequate justification within themselves, in their own relative nature"—or which at the worst, having reached "the extreme limit of its own platitude," degenerates into "the monstrosities of surrealism." Such art has the effect of dispersing and scattering the soul, while at the same time turning us in on our egos and thus away from God.

As we continue our journey, it is therefore essential that we be armed with criteria for distinguishing good from bad art. I realize, of course, that the moment I put the matter in so direct a way, many people are going to object that art is purely subjective, that it is a matter of taste alone. They will say that the expression of an artist's feelings or personal experience and the individual preferences of those who encounter his work are the sole determinants of what we may call its goodness or badness. According to this popular view, good art is a function of two things alone: the sincerity, originality, and intensity of the artist's perception, and the degree to which he is able to evoke in his audience a kind of sympathy by giving form to their own moods, expectations, or emotional needs.

Those who look at art in this way may well admit that certain artists have been quite pious men and that their art in some cases has been able to kindle a like piety in others. But an art which is only accidentally conducive to faith has no essential bearing on what the perennial philosopher means by the sacred. However religious its theme or content, such art has no necessary connection with the spiritual path. On the contrary, sacred art is art which points us toward God through the force of a quality or energy inherent in the form of the art itself, and independently of both the artist's individuality and our own personal likings or sympathies. It is intrinsically linked to the very structure of the universe, and it thus represents "an adequation to the Real." The Beauty of sacred art is no less objective than the Truth of metaphysical doctrine, the only difference being that "what the intelligence perceives quasi-mathematically, the soul senses in a musical manner that is both moral and aesthetic; it is immobilized and at the same time vivified by the message of blessed eternity that the sacred transmits."

As I acknowledged earlier, this is a very difficult point to explain, and it is difficult even for many religious believers to accept. I have been struck more than once by the indignation with which it is rejected by those who in every other way are attempting to lead a spiritual life, and by the tenacity and vehemence with which they cling to the notion that what they like in art could not possibly be harmful to their souls. Short of obscenity or pornography, these aesthetic subjectivists insist on a man's right to surround himself with the art of his choice, and they have no hesitation in filling even their sanctuaries with whatever strikes their personal fancy or seems most in keeping with the times. They do not understand that "in order that spiritual influences might be able to manifest themselves without encumbrance, they have need of a formal setting which corresponds to them analogically. Without this they cannot radiate, even if they remain always present." Of course, "it is true that in the soul of a holy man they can shine in spite of everything, but not everyone is a saint, and a sanctuary is constructed to facilitate resonances of the spirit, not to oppose them."

Perhaps you are an aesthetic subjectivist yourself. If so, allow me to remind you that nothing I may say, or that anyone says, will be able to convince you to the contrary. Beauty is meant to speak to us at a level deeper than words. Its impact is "direct and existential; it goes beyond thought and seizes our being in its very substance." It must be allowed to plead in its own defense. Hence only practical experience is going to provide you with the needed proof. Only through regular, living contact with the artistic forms authorized by a sacred tradition will you be able to verify for yourself that such forms "originate first and foremost from the same supra-human source from which all tradition originates," that they are meant above all for the sensible "transmission of intellectual intuitions" and as "a direct aid to spirituality," and that "authentic and normative art" must be based accordingly upon "rules that apply the cosmic laws and universal principles to the domain of forms." In the meantime, and in order to encourage you to begin that experiment, I would like to summarize these rules, the rules or criteria of sacred art, and to sketch very briefly how such art can elevate us in the direction of God.

The rules are basically three. "An art is sacred, not through the personal aims of the artist, but through its content, its symbolism, and its style, that is, through objective elements."

The perennial philosophy insists, first, that art is to be judged by "nobility of content." In order to be considered sacred, the content of a given piece of art must be canonically determined by a religious tradition, which establishes the limits within which the artist may work and provides him with appropriate subjects and themes. Like holy scripture, though "at very different degrees," sacred art is "derived from Revelation" and is "inseparable from inspiration." Because of its celestial origin, such art is well suited as a complement to anagogy, which is the mystical or spiritual exegesis of scripture. Together they assist in the transmission of doctrine by unfolding the hidden meaning of sacred texts. Scripture is "the direct expression of the Speech of Heaven, while anagogy is its inspired and indispensable commentary; art constitutes as it were the extreme limit or material shell of the tradition and thus, by virtue of the law that extremes meet, rejoins what is most inward in it."

The second rule or criterion is "exactness of symbolism." I have already explained that symbols are much more than just conventional signs. They are consubstantial with the realities in which they participate and toward which they lead us. It follows that "symbolism is a real and rigorous science," although of course one which "transcends the physical and psychic planes and thus is situated beyond the domain of methods termed scientific" in contemporary usage. As mentioned before, this symbolic science is closely tied to traditional cosmology and hence to the qualitative aspects of things understood as theophanies. "The science of symbols proceeds from the qualitative significances of substances, forms, spatial directions, numbers, natural phenomena, positions, relationships, movements, colors, and other properties or states of things; we are not dealing here with subjective appreciations, for the cosmic qualities are ordered in relation to Being and according to a hierarchy which is more real than the individual." The objectivity and universality of symbols mean that sacred art is able to transmit simultaneously metaphysical truths, archetypal values, historical facts, spiritual states, and psychological attitudes. One senses this range especially in "the multiform Beauty of a sanctuary," which is like "the crystallization of a spiritual flux or of a stream of blessings. It is as though invisible and celestial power had fallen into matter—which hardens, divides, and scatters—and had transformed it into a shower of precious forms, into a sort of planetary system of symbols, surrounding us and penetrating us from every side." If one looks along sacred forms and not simply at them, one begins to realize that each color, each line, each spatial relationship contains several levels of meaning, for "what is exteriorized in such art is both doctrine and blessing, geometry and the music of Heaven." I have so far put the matter in strictly visual terms, but the same thing is true, perhaps even truer, of auditory Beauty, which is to visual Beauty what essence is to form, and which also communicates at several degrees of depth. "Music is interiorized formal Beauty as formal Beauty is exteriorized music," and as such, music immediately draws us into its inward meanings. In any case, this dimension of depth comprising multiple levels of significance is what makes sacred art, whatever the medium, accessible to many different kinds of men, provided they approach it in a spirit of respect. This qualification is crucial, for the outward virtues embodied in sacred art can be discerned only by those in whom the inward beauties of humility, charity, and veracity have at least begun to blossom.

Whatever its level or mode, the presence of the sacred calls for reverence and submission on the part of man. In the actual making of sacred art, this submission takes the form of artistic anonymity, and this brings us to the third and final criterion: the importance of style. If a man is to become a fit medium for the transmission of Truth, his human poverty or emptiness must be offered up in order that the Divine may fill it. Such an offering is made possible by the artist's self-effacement before the masters of the style which he means to imitate. Only thus can he learn the essential rules of his art—rules concerning such elements as the correct proportions of figures, the proper clothing of sacred personages, the traditional representation of hieratic gestures, and the appropriate treatment of various materials such as wood, stone, and metal. These rules all reflect "the discipline or inspiration of a genius that surpasses" the individual artist himself, but which he attempts to approximate by faithfully copying the work of those to whom he has apprenticed himself. In this way, the artist is able to set himself and his own viewpoint aside so that the materials with which he works may speak on their own behalf. He is taught that whatever he is making, whether it is an icon or a piece of furniture, the work must formally express its proper use and that his treatment of the material he is using must be consistent with the intrinsic properties of the material and the object's intended function. Above all, "there must be no conflict between the essential and the accessory, but a hierarchical harmony," and this means that "if there be an added symbolism, it must conform to the symbolism inherent in the object," for "the object must not give an illusion of being other than what it really is." Only by respecting the implacability of stone, or the warmth and kindliness of wood, or the hostility and aggressiveness of iron does the artist provide a clear and proportionate passage for the objective qualities manifest in these natural substances. So also with colors, which may not be chosen at random. Sacred art must take account of the fact that "red excites, awakens, and 'exteriorizes'; blue gathers and 'interiorizes'; and yellow rejoices and 'delivers'"—to give just a hint of a much larger subject.

All three of these criteria—content, symbolism, and style—are woven very closely together, and all are directed toward a single goal, which is to open a window or passage. Sacred art is on a small scale what the world itself is on a large scale. The entire cosmos is a window if we would only look, and authentic art should be a window within this window, a place where clarity of vision may come a little easier. But vision of what? Windows are not the same as mirrors, and for this reason art should not show us ourselves. Hence the anonymity of the traditional artist, who deliberately eschews self-expression. But neither is a window the same thing as a photograph, which is why sacred art also avoids aesthetic naturalism—that is, the attempt to produce "a literal copy of the phenomena of nature." These phenomena are windows already, inherently translucent, and to copy them is to make them opaque. In order for art to assist in the transmission of spiritual light, rather than obstructing it, "man must imitate the creative act, not the thing created." This requirement does not imply that the artist should ignore the natural world. The world is made by God and must in all things be honored. But at the same time, the essential reason for sacred art is to get behind the effects to their Cause. It is designed to point, not to the world as such, but to what the world itself points toward, to that invisible Reality which the world reflects. This it can do only by in a certain fashion pointing away from that world. Sacred art "operates by abstraction in order to extract gold from 'raw material,'" and this is accomplished by combining "intelligent observation of nature with noble and profound stylizations in order, first, to assimilate the work to the model created by God in nature and, secondly, to separate it from physical contingency by giving it an imprint of pure spirit, of synthesis, of what is essential."

Many illustrations could be mentioned. The one with which I am most familiar, from my own tradition, is the Byzantine icon. Here one sees a striking example of what is meant by sacred art. Consider, for instance, certain icons of the Virgin Mary. The content is quite clearly traditional and canonical. One sees the Virgin's humility and tenderness in the slight declination of her head, while the inviolability and strength of the *Magnificat* are also evident in the nobility of her expression. The exactness of the symbolism appears in the circular shape of the nimbus surrounding her head. In having no end, the geometrical form of the circle conveys an essential quality of the celestial order. As for the artistic style, this is said traditionally to go back to St. Luke and the Angels, to whom the iconographer has submitted himself in his obedience to the instruction and example of his immediate teachers. One also notices what is meant by abstraction. While the icon is obviously a representation of a human person, the wideness of the Virgin's eyes, the small size of her mouth, and the relative size and evident authority of her Child are all unlike anything we would actually see in nature. Moreover the absence of visual perspective and of the illusion of depth reinforces our sense that what we are gazing upon is not to be found in this world. Our vision is not to be captured within the work itself, but should be directed instead through and beyond it to the supra-formal archetypes in which it participates. "Thus the icon, in addition to the beatific power that is inherent in it by reason of its sacramental character, transmits the holiness or inner reality of the Virgin and hence the universal reality of which the Virgin herself is an expression; in suggesting both a contemplative experience and a metaphysical truth, the icon becomes a support of intellection."

I strongly encourage you to take advantage of such supports. There is a celestial potency in these sacred forms that will many times reward your most prayerful attention.

❖ Chapter 18 ❖

The Practice of Beauty

Since Beauty is the expression of Truth, it is necessary to be attentive to Beauty on all planes.

*L*ike Truth and Virtue, Beauty is necessary for the spiritual life. But what exactly does this mean when it comes to the actual conduct of our lives? Virtue, we said, is fundamentally a state of being, but at the same time, it was important to mention certain particular virtues—humility, charity, and veracity—whose faithful practice can lead us to a recovery of that state. Beauty, too, is a dimension of Being itself. It is the place within sensible forms where they are pierced by the radiation of the Infinite and through which they may draw us back in the direction of God. With this in mind, we learned that the world as such is Beauty, and that in the human body and sacred art, this Beauty is drawn to an especially powerful focus. And yet we need to go further. You have come asking for advice, and as I observed at the start of our discussions, a satisfactory response to this request must provide some direction at the level of both theory and practice. Truth is conveyed by metaphysical theory, while Virtue, Beauty, and Prayer are all concerned with the methodical or practical application of this theory. From a different point of view, however, Virtue, Beauty, and Prayer themselves have both a theoretical and a practical dimension. In each case one may ask not only what the essential ingredient is, but what one is to do about it. It is not enough, for example, to know that Beauty is a revelation or theophany, nor even that it may be encountered in the body and art. We also need some concrete advice on how to bring Beauty into our day to day lives.

As I have pointed out before, Beauty occupies a unique place among the essentials of the spiritual life. Unlike Truth, Virtue, and Prayer, which are intrinsically necessary to our journey toward God, Beauty is extrinsic, being essential in fact though not in principle. The fact which makes it essential is the modern world. In a traditional civilization, the question of Beauty need never arise, or not at least with the same urgency. In such a world, "every formal element is a gift from Heaven," including even the simplest of crafts, and this "constitutes a pre-existent basis" for the spiritual way. "In the modern world, on the contrary, this basis practically no longer exists; the individual must consequently be aware of this problem and keep an eye on the formal integrity of his ambience in order to avoid as far as possible the presence of forms that are contrary to the Truth, the Path, and Virtue."

Ambience in this case includes everything with which we are surrounded, for "there is nothing that can or should remain outside the Path," however small or apparently insignificant. If we wish to draw closer to God, it is necessary to make sure, to the extent we can, that whatever we come into contact with is compatible with the Divine presence. This does not mean that God can be excluded from certain environments, or that He is somehow too dainty or pure to tolerate ugliness. "Doubtless one can be perfect, or tend towards perfection, in any formal context." But it does not follow that one may therefore "choose just any formal context in view of perfection. One may not renounce God on account of a spiritually unfavorable condition imposed on us by the world," but neither should a person "deliberately opt for an unfavorable condition while sincerely desiring God; in other words, one must not accept such a condition when it can be avoided." The Beauty of one's ambience is indispensable precisely to the extent that it can be realized in practice. We must strive for a balance that avoids both an obsessive perfectionism and a cynicism or slovenliness which thinks that anything is permitted.

The most important key is conformity with the natural environment. You should try to make sure, within whatever the realistic limits are in your case, that the materials, colors, and kinds of things in your ambience are as consistent as possible with the simplicity, humility, and dignity of nature. "Exiled on earth as we are, unless we are able to content ourselves with that shadow of Paradise that is virgin nature, we must create for ourselves surroundings which by their Truth and their Beauty recall our heavenly origin and thereby also awaken our hope." The best way to do this is to make those surroundings as much like nature as possible. "In nature, each thing is entirely what it must be, and each thing is in its rightful place according to the laws of hierarchy, equilibrium, proportions, rhythms; freedom of form and movement is combined with an underlying coordination." This combination should be reflected in every aspect of our environment. What in nature occurs by an act not its own and unconsciously must be deliberately and consciously incorporated into what we permit to exist around us. Some may object that nature is not without harshness or seeming disproportion. They may point out that "the ancient hermits, notably the Desert Fathers, used to seek out the most desolate places in nature" for the practice of Prayer. No one has said, however, that Beauty is all sunshine and sweetness. The splendors of nature doubtless include the biting cold of winter and the frightening power of storms. But snow and thunder are far from ugly, and the "'desolate' spots" of the hermits and ascetics were "neither factory walls nor office furnishings." It is impossible for anything in nature "to lie outside the span of Beauty, for the simple reason that in virgin nature Beauty is everywhere, both in severity and softness." Nature shows us both holy poverty and spiritual childlikeness. On the other hand, "it is in the midst of his own artifices that man most easily becomes corrupted; it is they that make him covetous and impious." This being so, we are wise to do all that we can to make our ambience, in spite of its artificiality, as natural as possible.

You might not ordinarily think of things this way, but your ambience actually begins with your physical body. It is your closest or most immediate environment, and Beauty must be honored beginning there. How beautiful a person's body or face might be is not of course within his control, though he is to some degree responsible for "the manner of his aging." To this extent our attentiveness to Beauty is closely bound up with maintaining our health and physical vigor. But the Beauty of the body resides not only in its static appearance. It also involves such things as carriage and movement. "The sense of the sacred, by the very fact that it coincides with devotion, essen-

tially implies dignity," and this includes "dignity of bearing, of ges-
ture; external comportment, which belongs to the moving periphery,
must bear witness in this periphery to the 'Motionless Center.'" Our
posture and outward comportment manifest our inward character,
for "the heart is revealed in gestures." At the same time, the outward
can subtly influence the inward. Through dignified action, we may
come in time to acquire a noble character. "It is in the nature of
man—since he combines the outward with the inward—to make use
of sensory supports towards the progress of his spirit or the equilibrium of his soul." Beauty does not produce Virtue, but "it favors in a
certain way a pre-existing Virtue."

Then there is the matter of how we dress and adorn our bodies. It
is quite remarkable how utterly indifferent most of our contemporaries seem to be to their clothing. Many people whose rectitude we
have no reason to doubt, and whose character we may even admire,
seem nevertheless completely oblivious to their appearance. The
rule once again should be consistency or conformity with nature.
"Prior to dress there was the naked body," and our clothing should
therefore "express or prolong the sacred character, the nobleness,
and the Beauty of the body." Sloppiness should be eschewed at all
costs, for "spirituality has an aristocratic air by definition," which is
fundamentally opposed to the "democratizing untidiness" of our
times. The modern world "denies Beauty on all planes precisely
because it expresses the Truth," and it does this in part by persuad-
ing us to reduce everything to the least common denominator. Aris-
tocracy, however, is not the same thing as an artificial formality.
Powdered wigs and lace were in their own day just as unnatural as
the opposite extreme is in ours. Dignity and simplicity go hand in
hand. The most important thing to remember is that "nothing in our
bodily appearance ought to be rendered contrary to the creative
intention of God." This implies, among other things, a difference in
clothing between the sexes, for how men and women dress should
reflect the different messages of their respective forms. Whether
man or woman, how you clothe yourself should express human
Beauty, but in a way which like all Beauty points back to God. This
means, for example, that we should choose "colors that are natural,
happy, calm," for like icons, we are not to call attention to ourselves,
but to be translucent. The popular fashion of wearing clothing
emblazoned with words and pictures must for this reason be carefully avoided. God did not make you to be a billboard for an advertis-

ing campaign. No matter the image you might happen to be wearing, it can only distract from the image you are.

Moving further out from the center, one comes next to the ambience provided by one's home. What dress is to nudity, one's dwelling is to the natural environment. Just as dress is there to express God's intention for the body, so one's "habitation must express or prolong the sacred character, the nobleness, and the Beauty of virgin nature." This rule applies to everything in one's home, from the materials that are used in its construction to the furnishings that are placed inside. Allowance must again be made, of course, for what is realistically possible. But given a choice, one should choose wood rather than either metal or plastic, and stone or brick rather than concrete, which is "a base and quantitative sort of counterfeit stone." One also looks for colors that are compatible with our natural surroundings. "Every element of Beauty or harmony is a mirror or receptacle which attracts the corresponding spiritual presence to its form or color." This principle applies most directly to sacred art and liturgical symbols, but "it is also true, in a less direct and more diffuse way, in the case of all things that are harmonious and therefore true. Thus, an artisinal ambience made of sober Beauty attracts or favors *barakah*": that is, blessing, grace, or spiritual presence. "Not that it creates spirituality any more than pure air creates health, but it is at all events in conformity with it." If you have the means, it is good to ornament your home with sacred art, or in any case with art and crafts produced according to traditional principles. But if not, it is much better to leave it empty and the walls bare than to burden and confuse your senses with just anything.

We have several times, and for several reasons, had occasion to cite the maxim that "one must know how to put each thing in its place." I hope you can see that this is not only a metaphysical axiom but a practical rule, or rather that it is a rule precisely because it is first an axiom. Your dwelling should be a sanctuary in which everything works together in disposing your soul to Prayer. It should be a garden or oasis in the midst of life's turmoil where movement toward God is unimpeded by the world's noise and distractions. If this is to happen, however, attention must be given to such basics as neatness and organization. We want to do all that we can to provide our senses with external supports for our journey, but this is quite impossible in the middle of clutter. At the very least, a space should be set aside in your home that is used exclusively for Prayer. Even just a corner will do, but this corner must be kept clean and neat and as beautiful as possible.

Clutter, of course, can be more than just visual. The word may be applied by extension to other aspects of the environment. A serious seeker should do everything possible, for example, to monitor what music he permits to enter his soul, for much of what passes for music today is at best auditory clutter. He is also going to have to avoid the radio and television almost entirely. He should be very cautious, too, concerning the reading with which he stocks his mind. This point applies in the first place to newspapers and magazines, but the rule extends to books and other reading materials in general, which also in a sense form a part of our ambience or environment. I am certainly not saying that you must give up informing yourself in due measure as to the state of the world, but as you know, a large part of what comes to us in the guise of information is at best unnecessary, and at worst inimical to the inward peace needed for the spiritual life. As for books such as novels, one should avoid "all the narrations that are fantastic, grotesque, lugubrious, 'dark,' thus satanic in their way, and well fitted to predispose men to all excesses and all perversions." The spiritual aspirant must "readily dispense with these somber lunacies," and this "without fearing in the least to be 'childlike' or caring in the least to be 'adult.'" Once again, simplicity is the key, and conformity with what might be called the naiveté, the spontaneity, and the innocence of virgin nature.

Our bodies, our dress, our homes and their furnishings, what we read and listen to—all of these are part of our ambience. So also are the words we use and the tasks we perform, and the other people to whom we relate. Each time we speak or carry out a task, however simple, we are creating a kind of psychic ambience, and this has its effect not only on ourselves but on those with whom we speak and work: our families, our professional colleagues, and friends. I have so far been discussing the subject of ambience as an aid to one's own spiritual efforts, but the appearance of our persons and homes, and our comportment in general, is not without significance for our neighbor as well. Giving attention to such things as dress and furnishings is a kind of charity, for "we owe it to others to show them, as far as possible, that we do not stop short at their earthly accidence, but that on the contrary we wish to take cognizance of their heavenly substance." Respect for other people "excludes all triviality in social behavior," for "politeness is a distant manner of helping our neighbor to sanctify himself." It also excludes triviality and careless-ness in our speech. "When one speaks, it is advisable to know in advance and as a matter of principle: what one says, why one says it, how one says it, to whom one says it, at which moment one says it." Not that our words should become artificial or stilted. One should also beware of a mere formalism taking pride in itself or putting on airs. But the point is that whenever we speak, we are placing a cer-tain demand on our listeners, using up time which they might have spent otherwise, perhaps in Prayer, and we therefore owe it to them to make sure that this time is not wasted. Above all, "God asks of us that we communicate to others the Truth," and "Truth must be enun-ciated, not only with a sense of proportion, but also according to a certain rhythm. One cannot speak of sacred things 'just anyhow.'" It is important to remember that the ways in which we can communi-cate or manifest the Truth are not confined to our speech or writing. We also "radiate through good example: through the virtues and so through the perfection of our activities," through the "subjective and objective rectitude of our work."

Our ambience is in part how we radiate, how we relate to other people. But it is also, finally, those people themselves. To be attentive to the Beauty with which we surround ourselves includes attention to the kinds of people with whom we associate. In many cases, we have no choice in such matters. There are our professional associ-ates, the people with whom we must work. And there are those whom destiny simply places before us, people with needs or prob-lems or questions that we are called to attend to, without consider-ation for who they are and whether they share our perspective and goals. Apart from a special vocation, most of us are obliged to live in a complex network of relationships with all kinds of people, and this certainly has its importance in teaching us such virtues as patience and resignation, not to mention simply courtesy and good manners. But at the same time, there is also room in our lives for more delib-erate associations, for seeking out people who like us are intent upon the spiritual life. What the Hindus call *satsanga*, an "association with saints" and "the frequenting of men of ascending tendency," is an important part of establishing an appropriate environment for Prayer, and I advise you to take it very seriously.

These few observations only touch the surface. But I have said enough, I think, to give you some sense of the many practical dimen-sions of Beauty. The essential principle is really very easy. In any given case, you must learn to ask yourself whether the book you are reading, the music you are listening to, the clothes you are wearing, the company you are keeping, and the home you are living in provide a congenial space for meeting God. If God were all at once with all His Beauty right there in the midst of your life, would these various things be destroyed or enhanced, abolished or perfected—condemned or taken up into glory?

Prayer

Men ought always to pray.

—Luke 18:1

✤ Chapter 19 ✤

Movement toward God

After simplicity, complexity; and after complexity, simplicity.
The Means, then its Modes; the Way, then the Goal. The one
after the other, but at the same time, the one within the other.

*Y*ou came for advice on the spiritual life. As I explained at the
outset, it seemed to me from how the question was posed that
you were looking for more than a superficial or formulaic response.
An effective answer would have to be one which took account of both
theory and practice—one that provided both an exposition and a
defense of essentials. As a result, you have been obliged to make
your way through some rather difficult pages, and to bend your
mind to the nuances of many distinctions. I realize that the going
has not always been easy, and I commend you for your perseverance
in staying with me to this point.

I hope that I have not attempted too much or made things unnec-
essarily hard to understand. For whatever else happens, I do not want
you to go away thinking that the spiritual life is only for those who
have mastered a technical vocabulary. The spiritual life is for everyone. If some people can enter upon that life only on the basis of various
distinctions and concepts, this is more a reflection of the differences
in human nature than the indication of some difficulty, certainly any

141

conceptual difficulty, intrinsic to spirituality itself. For "the Path is simple; it is man who is complicated," and some of us, it seems, are more complicated than others. The fact that I have been able to write all of this and that you have been able to read it is not something we ought to take pride in. We should realize instead that "metaphysical knowledge and holy childlikeness must go hand in hand," for "what separates man from Divine Reality is but a thin partition: God is infinitely close to man, but man is infinitely far from God."

The child in you will be happy to learn that we are nearing the end of this complex exposition. We have come to the last of the essential ingredients in our reunion with God, the element of Prayer. Practically speaking, Prayer is quite simply the most important thing in life. This is why the spiritual teacher can say that "even if our writings had on average no other result than the restitution for some of the saving barque that is Prayer, we would owe it to God to consider ourselves profoundly satisfied." If I have saved Prayer for last, this is not because of any secondary or derivative character, but because its very importance requires that one first carefully prepare the ground. Prayer is our prime means to that end which is God, but "it is useless to confer a spiritual means on a man without having first of all forged in him a mentality that will be in harmony with this means." Just as when a great king comes to town, with his entrance preceded by heralds and fanfare, so it is here in our preparation for Prayer.

On the one hand, Prayer is a name for the spiritual life as a whole. When you asked for my advice, I could have dispensed with all these many hundreds of sentences and said simply, Pray. For Truth, Virtue, and Beauty are all woven into the fabric of Prayer. No one can pray without knowing the true, doing the good, and loving the beautiful, while from the opposite end of the spectrum, we could say with equal propriety that this knowing, doing, and loving are all modes of praying. Prayer has been called "the meeting place of earth and Heaven." Whatever unites us with God must be a dimension of Prayer, whether the junction is doctrinal, moral, or aesthetic, and whether it comes about at the level of the Intellect, or the soul, or the body. For this reason it can be said that "the saint has himself become Prayer." In him, every level of the microcosm has entered upon its proper vocation. He has become the junction, and "thereby he contains the universe, and the universe prays with him. He is everywhere where nature prays, and he prays with her and in her:

in the peaks which touch the void and eternity, in a flower which scatters its scent, or in the carefree song of a bird."

As we are using the term in these discussions, however, Prayer is a name for a part, not the whole. I have compared it to our progress toward a goal. The spiritual life is a movement from Truth toward Truth, and this passage takes place in a context made possible by Virtue and Beauty. True theory or doctrine is our essential foundation, and the verification or realization of that Truth is our ultimate aim. This goal could not be reached, however, were it not for Virtue, which is inward Beauty, and Beauty, which is outward Virtue. These provide us with the indispensable space. They assist in clearing our path by displacing those things which would otherwise obstruct our progress. And yet Virtue and Beauty are not themselves that progress, nor is Truth the same thing as our movement in its direction. Motion is something distinct from the space in which it takes place and distinct as well from both our point of departure and our goal. If we mean to approach God in fact and not simply in theory, an operative or transformative element must be added to the picture, an element of method or spiritual discipline, and this is precisely what is supplied by Prayer. Up to this point, we have been dealing in a sense with preliminaries or prerequisites. Now we come to the heart of our endeavor. Only now can we really embark on the way.

I have several times paused to take note of various objections and criticisms. Responding to skeptics seemed especially important in the early stages of our conversation, for as I explained to you then, virtually all of us have been reared in an atmosphere of doubt and cynicism, and careful attention to this fact must form a part of our elementary spiritual education. My position throughout has been that the way of knowledge is especially suited to this education, that "only esoteric theses can satisfy the imperious logical needs created by the philosophic and scientific positions of the modern world." At the same time, however, I have also been trying to deal fairly with the concerns of religious believers who find themselves troubled or confused by an esoteric approach to the spiritual life. Metaphysical teachings, if encountered outside their proper context, cannot but seem scandalous from the bhaktic perspective. I have therefore done my best to explain them in a way which makes clear their essential difference from various contemporary counterfeits and pseudo-religions. I hope that by now there will be no mistaking authentic *gnosis* for gnosticism.

In considering Prayer, I shall continue to speak with a variety of listeners in mind. Presumably most of the skeptics fell away some time ago. But if any remain, or if there remains a skeptical voice within you yourself, I would hasten to point out that it is only Prayer which can finally and definitively satisfy any lingering wish for demonstration or proof. We looked at several proofs early on, and in a sense, the entire discussion of Beauty was meant to provide a tangible and all-pervasive proof of God for anyone with eyes to see. But nothing we have said can give such eyes to the man who does not have them. Prayer, however, can. "Prayer—in the widest sense—triumphs over the four accidents of our existence: the world, life, the body, and the soul; we might also say: space, time, matter, and desire." Prayer can bring us back into a living contact with Truth. It can restore a lost vision by piercing these several veils, by cutting through all that would capture attention and deflect it from the Divine Reality. In this way Prayer "puts us into the presence of God. It is like a miraculous diamond which nothing can tarnish and nothing can resist." A diamond of course must be used if we wish to cut something with it and not simply admire its brilliance. The skeptic may still object that in order to put Prayer into practice, he must first take seriously precisely what he continues to doubt. There is no merely theoretical way out of this dilemma. It is like the famous paradoxes of Zeno, which as the ancients said could be solved only by the action of walking, not just by more thinking. The same thing is true when it comes to the method of the natural sciences, so much vaunted in our day as the touchstone of objective truth. There, too, theories must be accepted in a provisional way so as to be tested by experiment. In no case can a man stand aloof, outside the laboratory of actual practice, if he really wishes to understand the nature of things.

But it is more to believers than to doubters that I shall be speaking below. The faithful man will obviously have no objection to the practice of Prayer. On the other hand, he may resist the emphasis which our teachers place upon it. We touched on this point in a somewhat different form earlier when speaking about the virtue of charity. I pointed out that the contemplative life is often thought to be a selfish affair, as if a man's vertical relationship with God were in a kind of competition with his horizontal relationship with his neighbors. As you know, ours is an age of social activism, and the conviction that Prayer is the most important thing in life is bound to seem disproportionate to many of our contemporaries, even the religious among them. They fail to understand that "the equilibrium of the world has need of contemplatives," that only "inwardness" is "capable of regenerating the world," and that "the world would have collapsed long ago but for the presence of the saints, be they visible or hidden."

These are claims once again which no one can prove to someone else, not at least empirically or discursively. And yet they follow ineluctably from all we have said about the centrality and deiformity of the human state and about the metaphysical unity of Reality. For "what is realized in the microcosm radiates in the macrocosm by reason of the analogy between all cosmic orders. Spiritual realization is a kind of 'magic' which necessarily communicates itself to the surroundings." By praying, I not only ready myself to be of service to others. I am of service precisely by praying. The inward and the outward are intimately, though invisibly, linked. An effective change within me inevitably has repercussions in my environment. It is certainly true that yours is the only soul you can save. But its salvation is at the same time the greatest possible act of love you will ever perform for your neighbor. Acquire inner peace, a saint has said, and thousands around you will find their salvation. Only in Prayer, which brings us face to face with the Absolute, are we able to distinguish on the plane of the relative between what is truly essential and all those many accidents which under the pretext of a presumed importance would bind us even more tightly to the ego. "The 'man of Prayer' is capable of measuring what he is able to offer to his ambience, and what he is able to accept from it, without dispersing himself and without being unfaithful to his vocation of inwardness; nothing should be to the detriment of our relationship with immanent Heaven. Only those who give themselves to God can know what they have a right, or duty, to give to the world and to receive from it." However one looks at the matter, no other practice is as important as Prayer.

"I am myself, and not someone else; and I am here, such as I am; and this necessarily occurs now. What must I do? The first thing that is obligatory, and the only thing that is obligatory in an absolute fashion, is my relationship with God. I remember God, and in and through this remembrance, all is well, because this remembrance is God's. Everything else lies in His hands."

Chapter 20

Faith

There is certainly a bhakti *without* jnana, *but there is no* jnana *without* bhakti.

*B*efore we proceed to a discussion of spiritual method as such, it is important to spend some time correcting what may have been a certain imbalance in my presentation thus far.

In the interest of stressing the distinctive nature of metaphysics or *gnosis*, I have several times called attention to the differences between esoterism and exoteric religious belief. Where the former finds its motivation in knowledge, the latter is sustained by devotion and love. Where the one takes note of distinctions in the Divine between Essence and Person, between the Absolute and the relative Absolute, the other is content to address itself to the Person alone. Where the one speaks of Virtue as an intrinsic state of being which must be recovered, the other thinks of Virtue as something to be attained by extrinsic actions. Where the one emphasizes the primordial perfection and theomorphism of man as such, the other concerns itself with the sinfulness of the individual man. And where the one delights in Beauty as the immanent presence of God, the other tends to be focused on the transcendence of God, and its attitude toward Beauty is therefore often one of indifference or even hostility. I am simplifying our earlier, more elaborate discussions and neglecting certain subtle but important nuances. Basically, however, these are the decisive points at which *gnosis* and exoteric belief part company.

But I must not leave you with the impression that the metaphysician is therefore disdainful of trust and piety. Nothing could be further from the truth. To take note as he does of the limitations of exoteric belief or to criticize the formulations of certain theological authorities is not at all the same thing as denying the importance of faith. We are taught on the contrary that even "the elect in Paradise necessarily have faith," for faith is essentially "a 'yes' from the depths of the soul, or from the entire soul, or from the heart—an inward, profound, and total 'yes' to the One who is both absolute and infinite, transcendent and immanent." If this is the case for those who are already in Heaven, all the more is it true for those still in this world, including even the greatest of sages. The truly wise man is the first to admit that "faith is not contrary to *gnosis*." He realizes that "not all faith is metaphysical knowledge," but at the same time he sees that "all metaphysical knowledge, being an 'evidence of things not seen,' is of the domain of faith," and that this faith "combines with *gnosis* in the depths of our being," since "knowledge does not abolish faith, but gives it a more inward meaning." In fact, one distinctive mark of the false teacher is any slightest suggestion that intellectual intuition can dispense with love and trust. "In view of the harm that the prejudices and tendencies of ordinary piety can sometimes do to metaphysical speculations," the esoterist may be "tempted to conclude that piety should be abandoned on the threshold of pure knowledge." But this is "a false and highly pernicious conclusion; in reality piety, or faith, must never be absent from the soul." The authentic master is always a man of great faith. The true *jnani* is always also a *bhakta,* and this is because "the love of God is the necessary complement of certitude, as the Infinite is the complement of the Absolute."

I could have stopped to stress this complementarity at any number of earlier points, for faith in fact must work together with all of the essential elements in the spiritual life. First of all, Truth. We have said that a man's intelligence is independent of the kind of man he is, since no one can know the false in the same way that he can choose the bad or love the ugly. Our capacity to discern the Truth cannot be perverted without its ceasing to be what it is, and in this sense the capacity is independent of faith. Nevertheless, faith is not for that reason expendable. Although we need not have faith for the apprehension of Truth, we do need it for the appropriation or assimilation of Truth. "He who 'knows' theoretically does indeed enjoy metaphysical certainty." He may be certain, for example, that God exists. "But such certainty does not yet penetrate his whole being; it is as if, instead of believing a description, one saw the object described, without the sight of it implying either a detailed knowledge or possession of this object, for one glance does not of course tell us the whole nature of the thing seen. Thus there is in this case certainty as to the object as such, but uncertainty as to its integral nature. Perfectly to 'know' the object means to 'possess' it, to 'become' it, to 'be' it. If the sight of an object is very much more than an abstract belief in its existence, the realization of the object will likewise be infinitely more than the sight of it." Here is where faith comes in. "If intellectual qualification is the discernment that is capable of passing from appearance to reality, from forms to essence, and from effects to cause, then faith is the propensity to pass from the concept to the thing itself, or from knowing to being." Faith is not "intellectual certainty," but it is "that something which makes intellectual certitude become holiness; or which is the realizatory power of certitude." To return to an earlier image, Truth without faith is to Truth with faith what the circle is to the sphere or the square to the cube.

Faith for the true gnostic is also closely connected with Virtue. "Faith is fidelity to the supernaturally natural receptivity of primordial man; it means remaining as God made us and remaining at His disposition with regard to a message from Heaven which might be contrary to earthly experience." You might wish to recall what was said about anonymity. Virtue, we learned, is not something that a man must strive to gain, or for which he can take the credit. His moral efforts should consist instead in eliminating those faults which mask the intrinsic virtues of his primordial nature, virtues existing on a level deeper than the plane of the fall and therefore deeper than the ego or individual being. On this level, man remains open to God, from whose qualities human virtues are borrowed. Faith is being open to that openness. "Faith demands the virtues and at the same time deploys them." One can see that this is so with regard to each of the fundamental virtues. Humility is fidelity to the transcendence of God as the Absolute. Charity is fidelity to the immanence of God as the Infinite. And veracity is fidelity to the transcendence of the Infinite in the midst of its immanence, and to the immanence of the Absolute in the face of its transcendence. Faith is a sense of proportions, a resilience before the kaleidoscopically shifting play in the nature of things. Humility is saying Yes to the unicity of the Real, charity is saying Yes to the totality of the Real, and veracity is saying Yes to the unity of the Real. In every instance, faith is essential.

The same point must be made when it comes to Beauty. In its widest sense, Beauty is what permits us to discern God in the world. It is what we see, and see by, when we become aware of "the metaphysical transparency of phenomena." But this awareness is itself woven of faith. I have called it a sense of the sacred. If faith is realization or assimilation in relation to Truth, and anonymity or conformity in relation to Virtue, it is the sense of the sacred in relation to Beauty, for "perfect faith consists in being aware of the metaphysically miraculous character of natural phenomena and in seeing in them, by way of consequence, the trace of God." There is no sense of the sacred without faith. But the reverse is true, too. The sacred is the food by which faith lives, and without it faith dies. "The sense of the sacred: this word felicitously expresses a dimension which should never be absent either in metaphysical thought or in everyday life; it is this which gives birth to the liturgies, and without it there is no faith. The sense of the sacred, with its concomitances of dignity, incorruptibility, patience, and generosity, is the key to integral faith and to the supernatural virtues which are inherent in it."

Faith is the substance of Truth, the gate to Virtue, and our repose in Beauty. Nevertheless I have saved an explicit consideration of faith until now because it is a subject even more intimately connected with Prayer. Prayer is our movement toward God. But faith is what makes that movement possible. It is the motive force behind every aspect of one's spiritual practice. I am of course using the term to mean a good deal more than just acceptance or assent alone. If faith meant only "an adherence of the sentiments" to the dogmatic forms propounded by a religious authority, or if it were simply the same thing as a belief "affectively centered on a credo," where "the volitive element predominates over the intellectual," then obviously faith would find itself at odds with esoterism and the way of knowledge. But faith signifies much more than this even for the exoteric believer. It is not just a case of "accepting without seeing," but of commitment and submission to what one has seen: "an attitude of calm, of trust, of resignation, of 'poverty,' of existential simplicity." Faith, we might say, is "the feminine element that is joined to the masculine element that is certitude." In this sense, faith involves "a quasi-ontological and premental certitude" concerning realities that escape an exclusively empirical perception, but which are nevertheless proven precisely by this faith itself. Faith can therefore be said to be "identical in its center with knowledge." In this "higher aspect," faith is the "*religio cordis*" or religion of the heart. "It is the 'inward religion' which is supernaturally natural to man and which coincides with *religio caeli*, or *perennis*"—the religion of the blessed in Heaven, the perennial religion—and hence "with universal Truth, which is beyond the contingencies of form and time."

Faith in this sense is crucial for the practice of Prayer. The way of knowledge accords at every stage with man's wish for certainty. It therefore never demands from him a blind assent to something for which no reason can be given. But it does demand fervor, aspiration, and a persevering intensity. "*Gnosis* transcends and abolishes faith, but only when faith is understood as a quasi-moral acceptance of revealed truths, and not as a concrete presentiment of the Inexpressible." Spiritual practice presupposes this presentiment, and it demands that man commit himself fully to become what he is. Faith is what can give him strength in that struggle. The fact that there is an Absolute, which cannot not be, and that this Absolute must be equally Infinite, since it is without any limits, requires from the man who knows it a continual investment of his total being—body and soul, together with Intellect. Faith is the force which brings this totality into play and keeps us focused from day to day on our goal. "Life is a chain of moments, and we can—and must—at every moment say 'yes' to the Divine Will." Of course, "this does not deliver us from the evils we must face in the outward world." But it does help to bring our thoughts and emotions, our choices and actions, into line with our intellectual discernment that such evils cannot but exist. In this way the Yes of faith can "deliver us from our passional reactions to these evils."

The movement toward God which is Prayer involves a liquefaction or melting, and faith is the fire which provides the needed heat. "Every spiritual path begins with an inversion with regard to the preceding state. The profane soul is in a state of 'hardness,' for it is closed to God who shines 'outside' it. This hardness reveals itself by indifference with regard to God and then by egoism, greed, anger, and distraction; consequently spiritual conversion will involve fervor, goodness, renunciation, and peace. The soul must 'melt' in the face of Truth, so that the Divine presence will henceforth be felt as 'inward' and 'central.'" We must come to a point "where there is no longer any hardness, no longer a constricting coil around the ego," to a place where "within there is bliss and outwardly there is goodness, and a gentle warmth like spring sunshine, comparable to the joy of love."

Faith is the sun that makes all of this possible.

⊰ Chapter 21 ⊱

Method and Grace

God is not arbitrary and does not refuse His grace to the soul that has put itself in the required state of readiness, just as nature does not refuse fire to wood that is dry and sufficiently heated by rubbing.

*Y*ou have understood the essential points of metaphysical doctrine and have a firm foundation in Truth. You have begun to cultivate the fundamental virtues by weeding out the vices which stand in the way of their full flowering. And you have taken steps to create for yourself, insofar as possible, an ambience of Beauty. What else should you do? I have said you must pray. It is time to be more precise as to just what Prayer includes, to speak about spiritual method or technique. How specifically are we to overcome the fallen tendencies which would draw us away from God?

We have pictured the spiritual journey as a movement through space. You would do well at this point to think of it as primarily a vertical motion, a motion working against the weight of the ego and the downward pull of passion and pride—of indolence, disquiet, and self-centeredness. Before we first embark on the path, we are entrenched in a state of "passional and blind affirmation" and of "spiritual laziness, inattention, dreaming." Our days are filled with "agitation, dissipation, and the contraction which is the static coun-

terpart of agitation," while at the same time we suffer from a "fragmenting of the soul among sterile facts, in their insignificant and
empty multiplicity, their desiccating drab monotony." In this state,
"the soul is both hard like stone and pulverized like sand; it lives
among the dead husks of things and not in the Essence which is Life
and Love." Above all, we suffer from "the congenital confusion which
attributes to the unreal the quality of the Real," and our view of ourselves is correspondingly distorted by "separative illusion, the error
of believing that I am identified with the empirical 'I' composed of
outward and inward experiences, mental images, and volitions."

Because of our passion and pride, and our agitation and laziness,
our spiritual efforts must include both negative and positive aspects.
The hot head must be cooled and the cold heart must be warmed. We
need to withdraw from the outward, but we also need to repose in the
inward. Our attachment to the world must in some way be severed
so that everything within us can then be focused on God. An adequate method or discipline will always include both these dimensions—dimensions reminding us once again of transcendence and
immanence. In the face of the Absolute, all the world is but vanity,
illusion, and nothingness, and we must at all costs extract ourselves
from the mortal grip of its accidents. But in light of the Infinite, all
the world is Divine, and it is to be honored and affirmed with a view
to its immortal Substance. To be absent from illusion so as to be
present to Reality: this is the essential aim of all method, for "when
man interiorizes himself, God exteriorizes Himself while enriching
man from within."

What exactly do I mean by negation and affirmation? What precisely should you do? Let us begin with the negative aspect of
method.

When it comes to cutting the cord of desire which binds us to the
world, perhaps the most important practice of all is the periodic
retreat. This word is often used to describe an extended time of
Prayer and reflection, but in using it here, I am referring to any
period of spiritual solitude, however short or long. Each of our hours,
each of our days, each of our years should be punctuated by regular
retreats. When discussing various practical rules under the heading
of Beauty, I spoke about the importance of setting aside a space for
Prayer. We need to establish a center if we mean to resist the centrifugal attraction of things around us. It is even more important, however, that we learn to set aside certain times for Prayer. We exist not

only in a world of phenomena and forms which would distract us from God, but also in the midst of time or duration, which "draws us along from birth unto death" and "continually wants to change us." Overcoming time, as you will quickly discover, is much harder than overcoming space. "It is in principle easy to withdraw into the Center and thus everywhere to leave space, but it is difficult to maintain oneself in the Present and thus to leave time at every moment." The present moment is "an almost ungraspable place," and yet grasp it we must, for the present is "a drop of eternity amid the ceaseless shiftings of forms and melodies," and in that moment we, too, "are already eternal."

For this we need considerable practice, however. In order to guarantee time for such practice, you will need to establish a rhythm of retreats. Every year at least one entire day should be designated for Prayer, and nothing but Prayer. No reading, no talking, no company, no music, no interruptions. And if possible no food, for fasting is a most helpful support for remembering God, commended by all traditional teachers. Similarly, you should develop the habit of withdrawing from the world at regular times every day. Certainly upon rising in the morning and again before retiring at night, one should make a point of resisting for a while the demands and din of daily life. It is also important to arrange your professional affairs in such a way that you can break away from them in the midst of each day, even if only for a very few minutes. Deliberately interrupting the flow of our activities, especially when they seem unusually pressing, can go a long way toward breaking the hold which the world has upon us. These daily retreats should once again be times of solitude when you can be completely alone with God. Finally, you should strive to turn every idle moment into a kind of miniature retreat. Those many wandering thoughts and daydreams which fill up the largest part of even our busiest hours are to be replaced by Prayer. You will not be able to provide for outward solitude in all of these cases, but if you have been disciplined as to your daily and yearly retreats, even these brief moments will become opportunities for that inward solitude which is detachment and spiritual poverty. You will begin to understand that "it is not Prayer which traverses time as it repeats itself; it is time which, so to speak, halts before the already celestial unicity of Prayer."

As for the affirmative or positive dimension of method, I would for the moment make just two suggestions, corresponding to the two levels of our individuality. If we are to change our orientation and become focused on God, it is crucial that measures be taken to involve the whole of our being in the life of Prayer. Man is a microcosm, and unless the several levels of this universe are properly ordered and working in concert, the improvement of any one of them will do us little good. We know that the Intellect is already in principle directed toward God. I shall be speaking shortly about how it may become operative in fact. In the meantime, what should be done with regard to the soul and the body?

As you will remember, the soul of man, using the term in its broader sense, includes three distinct elements: the intelligence, the will, and the sentiment. It is the seat of our thinking, our choosing, and our feeling. In order for the soul to be effectively united to God, something must be done to attract and hold the attention of each of these elements in a way that is consistent with their respective natures. The soul must be fed with a nourishment that can at once be thought, willed, and felt. This is the purpose of meditation. Meditation is meant to "contribute towards actualizing our receptivity" to God by "stimulating the pious imagination" and "by calling forth 'Platonic recollection.'" Perhaps you are familiar with certain forms of traditional meditative practice—for example, the Christian rosary, with its rhythmic rehearsal of the mysteries of Christ and the Virgin. By proposing ideas for reflection, meditation gives us something to think about, but in linking these ideas with evocative images, it is also able to stimulate the corresponding sentiments, and working together, our thinking and feeling gradually begin to draw in their wake the appropriate choices as we aspire to realize the attendant virtues. "Meditation acts on the one hand upon the intelligence, in which it awakens certain consubstantial 'memories,' and on the other hand upon the subconscious imagination, which ends by incorporating in itself the truths meditated upon, resulting in a fundamental and as it were organic process of persuasion."

Take a simple example. You may tell me that I should practice resignation or patience. But no matter how great my efforts in this direction, as long as my will is attempting to act in a vacuum, I shall see few results. If we are to get anywhere in such spiritual work, "it is a precious help to be deeply convinced both as to the things towards which we are tending, and also of our capacity to attain them, with the help of God." Deep persuasion means a combination of thought and sentiment. Suppose, therefore, that rather than simply commanding me to exercise patience, you instead explain this virtue in connection with the absoluteness of God, who cannot not be, and whose impassibility remains unaffected by the turmoil and disintegration of our world. And suppose that you asked me to picture a calm pool of water and to feel in my imagination how the passivity of the water toward its container allows it to remain always unbroken. If I made it my practice rhythmically to return to this constellation of ideas and images, while meditating at other times on the other qualities of God and their corresponding virtues, then eventually I might well learn to be patient. For "the result of persevering practice of comprehension by meditation is the inward transformation of the imagination or the subconscious, the acquisition of reflexes that conform to spiritual reality."

The body, too, must be involved in one's spiritual discipline. As we saw earlier, because of the law of inverse analogy, there is a correspondence between the spiritual or intellectual domain and its physical or corporal counterpart. For this reason, the body can be a more direct and immediate witness to spiritual realities than the soul. Its participation in Prayer is therefore an especially effective means to contemplative concentration. Prostrations, sacred gestures, and rhythmic breathing and chanting are just a few of the ways in which the body may enter into a spiritual regimen and assist in our efforts to remain focused on God. If you are attentive in times of solitude and quiet, you will discover moreover that there is a kind of consciousness or awareness in your "bodily substance" itself, which is "actualized in perfect immobility: the moment we do nothing but 'exist,' we are virtually identified with Being, beyond all cosmic coagulations." On the other hand, "concurrently with bodily consciousness, there is vital, energetical consciousness, in short, life and movement," together with "symbolic gestures," and these "can be vehicles for our participation in cosmic rhythms and in universal life, at all the levels that are accessible to us by virtue of our nature and through grace."

Finally, besides the body as such and its movement, there are the different regions of the body, each of which has a mode of awareness and a sensitivity or receptivity peculiar to itself. We referred to these before in connection with the Beauty of the human form. In this context, I would mention just two such domains: the forehead and the heart. "Man is like a tree whose root is the heart and whose crown is the forehead." The forehead contains our "mental space—the sub-

stance or energy containing or producing thought." When the auto-
matic succession of discursive thinking, the almost incessant chatter
of the mind, is stopped, the forehead "'thinks God' by its very substance, in 'holy silence.'" Visualization of symbolic forms can be a
powerful aid to Prayer, for "the visual image *a priori* addresses the
mind," and thus "it pertains to the region of the forehead." As for the
heart, it too can be "the support of an existential 'remembrance of
God'" because of its sensitivity to "evocative sounds" and "auditory
symbols," whether music or words. Whatever the corporal region
that is engaged, "all this enters into a psychosomatic alchemy of
which the spiritual traditions of the East offer us many examples,
and of which the Christian liturgies offer echoes," an alchemy which
reminds us once more that "the possibility of our return to God" is
"inscribed" in the "very nature of our existence."

In speaking of these more or less technical aspects of Prayer, it is
very important, however, that we do not start confusing spirituality
with mere technique. Method is not mechanical. While there do exist
certain powerful aids to concentration, their use does not provide
any guarantee of progress in the way. "All great spiritual experiences
agree in this: there is no common measure between the means put
into operation and the result. 'With men this is impossible, but with
God all things are possible,' says the Gospel." God is never effect, but
always cause. No matter what our efforts, His response will always
be a matter of gift and grace. Indeed without God, those very efforts
would be impossible, for "without grace man can do nothing even if
nourished with wisdom and filled with virtue."

Two opposite errors must be avoided. We see here yet another case
in which authentic *gnosis* makes its way between extremes. The first
error can be seen in the ideologies of self-improvement that are so
popular today. Everywhere a person turns, he is offered yet another
formula or program for developing his so-called spiritual potential.
If only you follow these steps or those rules, it is claimed, then you
are guaranteed to realize the benefits of a new and blissfully happy
life. The authentic teacher offers no such promises. He insists on the
contrary that "even the most penetrating intelligence, if it relies too
much on its own strength, runs the risk of being abandoned by
Heaven; forgetting that the Subject, the Knower, is God, it closes
itself to the Divine Influx." Part of the problem lies in the ambiguity
of this very word *Subject,* or its equivalent: the *Self.* The metaphysician is the first to agree that the real *I* is Divine and that the final

goal of the spiritual life is to realize our unity or identity with the Self. This Supreme Self or true *I*, however, is not the same thing as the ego which presumes to go by its name. And yet because of the ambiguity of the terms and the eagerness of many people to be deceived, the frauds and charlatans have an easy time making it seem as if spirituality were a matter simply of expanding the domain of our passions, and every ego is by definition only too happy to oblige them. What all such pretenders forget, or deliberately ignore, is that while "God resides in our deepest 'being,' or at the extreme transpersonal depth of our consciousness," and while "we can in principle realize Him with the help of the pure and theomorphic Intellect," we are nonetheless obliged to admit "the equal and simultaneous affirmation of this immanent and impersonal Divinity as objective and personal." The infinity of God, in other words, is never to the exclusion of His absoluteness, nor is His Essence to be realized apart from His Person. I shall say more about this last, most crucial point in our final meditation. For the moment it is enough to emphasize that "we can do nothing without grace, despite the essentially 'Divine' character of the Intellect in which we participate naturally and supernaturally." You should therefore avoid any path that purports to reach Heaven by technique alone.

The second error consists in going too far in the opposite direction from spiritual effort, insisting instead upon an "absolute gratuitousness" that would end by making Prayer unnecessary. It has been said that without God man can do nothing. But it is also true that without man God will do nothing. Whatever efforts we make are pure grace, but they remain, as grace, our efforts, and must not be disparaged. I am returning in a sense to the mystery of freedom and predestination. It is true that one must avoid "replacing God" with the "'mechanical' factors of spirituality" or the "'technical' utility" of a method. At the same time we need to understand that an authentic "method is itself already a grace, being a free gift by the fact of its revelation, while at the same time being necessarily efficacious in its modes of working, like the sacraments." If grace and method were in no way connected, it would be "contradictory to speak of 'means of grace.'" If God had no use for man's efforts, there would be no sense in His having commanded them or in His having laid down certain rules as to their proper direction and operation. Certain religious believers will object to the stress I am putting on spiritual method on the grounds that salvation is the work of God alone. Where the

spiritual charlatans give too little to God, these well-meaning believers commit the opposite error of giving too little to man, to man's
efforts to practice Prayer as a method or discipline. Rightly fearful of
those who wish to achieve Heaven on their own terms, and who end
up confusing God with the ego, they often dismiss meditation and
the various bodily disciplines that I have alluded to as forms of an
objectionable "natural mysticism." Such people are right that "man
always remains passive in relation to grace." But what they fail to
see is that "grace and method are not antagonistic principles," but
rather "the two poles" of an indivisible, "single reality."

Man is indeed passive before God, but within this passivity, he is
to be active as well: "active in concentration" at the very least, and
in "all that is connected therewith, or, to put it summarily, in eliminating distractions." For we are to be doers of the word, and not hear-
ers only.

❧ Chapter 22 ❧

Concentration through Intention

The man who is chased by a bull flees without having to make an effort of concentration; the same holds good for lovers who make haste to meet; the efficacy, and so the concentration, is in the sincerity of the intention, and this depends on the reality of the situation.

*I*t is impossible to talk about Prayer without saying a few words on the subject of concentration. We have seen that spiritual discipline requires that the whole of our being become focused on the Divine Reality. Although we have pictured the spiritual life as a journey, its goal paradoxically is that we should remain always where we are. We should be here where God dwells at the center, not wandering along the periphery or at the circumference of things. And we should be here not sometimes but always, permanently in the present moment which opens onto eternity.

But how is this to be done? In a sense, our entire discussion thus far has been devoted to answering this very question, for uninterrupted union with God is impossible except on the basis of Truth and in a context provided by Virtue and Beauty. Metaphysical doctrine, intrinsic morality, and sacred aesthetics are all essential for contemplative discipline, and contemplative discipline in its turn is essential for union. Woven into our meditations on these basic elements, there have also been certain specific instructions, hints as to the preliminary steps a person needs to take if he seriously aspires to remain always at the center with God. These have included a description of the fundamental virtues, some rules to observe concerning one's dress and ambience, and most recently certain words of advice about the importance of making time for retreats.

But there is more to be said. Having established a spiritual discipline based upon these indications, you will quickly discover that the way has just begun. Fulfilling these precepts brings a man no further than the start of the path. The real work remains. It is one thing to turn away from the world, and this is relatively easy. It is somewhat harder so to order your daily life that you are able to persevere in this detachment, and yet this, too, can be managed by nearly everyone. The hardest thing of all, however, is yet to come. Having cut yourself off from the space around you and having disentangled yourself from the demands of time, you must now take the further step of overcoming the space and time that remain inside the soul itself. With a little effort, I can find a place that is quiet, and it is easy to close my eyes. But the images and sounds of the world will nonetheless continue to flash and resound within me. Similarly, I can make provision for the daily retreats and allow for regular times of Prayer. And yet even though I may be outwardly free from my professional schedule and other responsibilities, the distractions of time persist in my anticipation and memory. I find myself still "feverishly straining toward the future" and either "lovingly or sadly bent over the past." The future and the past continue to press upon me, crowding out "the pure present," which is "the moment of the Absolute," and in which alone I can truly "stand before God."

You do not need for me to list the many kinds of distraction. You know them all too well. Spend a few minutes trying to be attentive to just one thing, and you quickly discover that the mind is but smoke driven by wind. Ironically, the greatest distractions are those which are subtly connected to the spiritual life itself, grafted onto certain legitimate needs and efforts. The corruption of the best is the worst, they say, and this maxim pertains without doubt to contemplative practice. I shall mention just three of the forms which such distraction takes. There are far too many to catalogue here, but this brief summary should give you a sense of what to look out for.

One must be careful, first, that spiritual detachment does not become an excuse for bitterness or animosity. "Wishing to be alone

with God: the rightness of the intention requires that there be in this
desire for holy solitude no false note. One cannot wish to be alone
with God because one scorns men. This would amount to saying that
only God is good enough for us and that we do not belong to the
human species." Withdrawal and denial can all too easily become fer-
tile ground for arrogance and resentment, and to counter this tendency, "the soul isolating itself before God must have a feeling of
goodwill and respect towards its peers; it must have no feeling of personal superiority nor of scorn." It is an essential part of discernment
to realize that the world is evil, that it is the domain of desire, suffering, and death, and that it must therefore be renounced. But at
the same time a man should remember that "he is not alone in having this awareness, nor alone in loving God; nor, above all, is he
alone," whatever the degree of his solitude, "in being loved by God."

A second distraction is the false, and very dangerous, presumption that Prayer is a method of gaining something for ourselves. This
is perhaps the most common mistake of spiritual aspirants in our
day. It has always been possible to turn contemplative practice into
a means to a worldly end, and the traditions have consistently
warned against this temptation. But it seems to have been left to our
age, the so-called new age, to put a glossy face on this deviation and
to act as if satisfying the individual interests of the ego were the ultimate goal of human life. The desires which a man may seek to satisfy
range from the coarse to the refined, and it is the most refined that
become the most subtly interwoven into our practice and are the
most difficult to extirpate.

The coarsest of all is the ego's wish for "powers or other purely profane advantages." It is to this desire that many false teachers appeal.
The advantages may take the form of wealth or physical health and
prowess, or the "gift of miracles or the prestige of holiness." There is
also the desire simply for comfort, for a happiness that comes from
feeling at home in the world. How many schemes of spiritual fitness
are put forward as ways of coping with life, of overcoming tension
and producing relaxation? "For too many men, the criterion of the
value of life is a passive feeling of happiness which *a priori* is determined by the outer world; when this feeling does not occur or when
it fades, they become alarmed, and are as if possessed by the question: 'Why am I not happy as I was before?' and by the awaiting of
something that could give them the feeling of being happy." One of
our greatest temptations is the pernicious idea that if only we had

this, or if only we did that, then life would be unfailingly pleasant, and all our problems with the world would be solved. This sort of thinking may easily carry over into Prayer. Perhaps if I embarked on a spiritual way, then everything would be just the way I want. This, however, is "a perfectly worldly attitude," whatever its attempts to hide behind a spiritual facade. "The desire not to suffer injustices or even simply not to be disadvantaged" comes from forgetting that "on earth man is in exile; the very fact of death proves it." The serious seeker keeps this truth firmly in mind and refuses to let the ego's complaints dissuade him from his course. However many the apparent injustices to which he finds himself subject, he remembers that they "result from our past faults, and then our trials exhaust this causal mass," or they come from "our character, and then our trials bear witness to them. In both cases," he knows, "one must thank God and invoke Him with all the more fervor, without preoccupying ourselves with worldly chaff."

Yet another desire, perhaps the most tenacious of all, is the desire for graces, illuminations, spiritual degrees or consolations, and other signs of progress on the path. This brings me to a third kind of distraction, one to which it is closely connected: the distraction which comes from wishing to know where we stand in the eyes of God. Our authorities tell us that "all individual interest other than salvation is properly sacrilegious and can only have disastrous consequences." This includes even our interest in how well we are doing and how far we have gone—in short how good we are, spiritually speaking. Right intention or aim in the spiritual life eschews this interest completely. It therefore "excludes the expectation of immediate, or impending, or tangible results" that might serve to measure our improvement or growth, especially results of a supernatural kind, such as "inward joys or celestial visions or voices," or a "tangible knowledge of Divine mysteries." Such expectations are really a kind of "subtle worldliness," seeking confirmation in information or data. "Instead of being governed by phenomena and following inspirations," the aspirant must learn to "submit to principles and accomplish actions." He comes to realize that "what Heaven asks of us, or what it wishes to tell us, is to be found in necessary and certain things, not in things that are merely possible and moreover conjectural." Certainly, graces and inspirations may sometimes come our way. But even when they do, we should be careful that they do not become seductions.

It is very easy, for example, to turn a retreat that has seemed to us especially good, one where we have felt composed or alert or at peace, into a standard for all future times of Prayer. In this way the ego is able to keep us so fixed on the memory of our previous feelings and on the anticipation of their repetition that no room is left for God. "When a man experiences a spiritual state or a grace, or if he has a vision or an audition, he must never desire that it be produced again," and he must certainly not assume that "it has conferred any eminence whatever upon him. The only thing that counts is to practice what brings us closer to God, while observing the conditions that this practice requires; we do not have God's measures, and we do not need to ask ourselves what we are."

This last point is crucial. The entire aim of the spiritual life is to bring us into union with God. It is therefore very easy for the ego always to be looking in the mirror to see how well it is doing or how far it has gone. Comparing itself to others is merely the grossest form of this error. It is the concern for our individuality that is the problem, and not just the invidious comparisons resulting from it. Spiritual discipline must be a case of the left hand not knowing what the right hand is doing. Though we should seek to move closer to God, the motion itself must be ignored. To use a different image, "it is as if one were walking along a narrow path between two abysses." On the one side is the surrounding world which we are trying to leave behind, and on the other is the inward spiritual life that we have begun to cultivate. The seeker must beware of becoming so enamored with the latter that he forgets that neither the outer nor the inner as such is his goal. "When looking to either side one risks losing one's balance; one must, on the contrary, look straight ahead," maintaining a focus on God alone. Spirituality is a means, not the end. The precise quality or depth of our practice should be of no concern to us. "If in fact we are saints, that is of interest to Heaven, since Heaven is interested in our good; but our desire for sanctity could not be of interest to Heaven." In the final analysis, nothing is so great a distraction, nothing so stands in the way of realizing our full perfection in God, as an ambitious and passionate perfectionism, which is like "the wind which blows out the light of a candle."

So how does one avoid these distractions? How are we to concentrate on God alone? The answer lies in having a right intention or motive. "As regards concentration, which is the operative prolongation of knowledge, it is closely linked with intention, to the extent of having no value except through it. A man who powerfully practiced concentration with the intention of obtaining the gift of miracles or the prestige of holiness would gain nothing and lose everything; on the contrary, a man who failed to concentrate, despite the utmost good will, but who did so with a spiritually acceptable intention, would be accepted by Heaven." For "God listens to the intention of even the incapable," but He does "not accept the technical perfection of the ambitious and the hypocritical." This is because "the legitimacy of the intention produces in fact a sufficient concentration." We have looked at a few of the improper intentions for Prayer: animosity or scorn for others, the desire for power or worldly happiness, and the wish to be granted spiritual gifts or signs of sanctity. What are the acceptable reasons for Prayer? What is it that will allow us to concentrate?

There are three such reasons. "We can legitimately invoke God either to save our soul, or because we love the climate of the sacred, or again on account of metaphysical realities." In the first place, one's spiritual practice may be based upon a wish to be saved. Unlike the desires that we considered above, for privileges or powers that might call attention to the ego and bolster its pride, a true longing for salvation is rooted in humility, in man's recognition of his powerlessness, and in his wish to be rid of his vices and freed from his sins. This may be referred to as the intention of fear. Second, the life of Prayer may be based upon love—love of God, of course, but also on a delight in the joy of Prayer itself. We have said that a merely passive feeling of happiness is an illegitimate motive for Prayer. But the happiness which accompanies our spiritual efforts is altogether different, and this may well serve as a proper motive for seeking God. Total trust and confidence in Divine mercy are worlds apart from a listless expectation of comfort, and this trust may give rise to a kind of weightlessness or insouciance, "like a bird which sings or like a child at play." Praying because one delights in such songs or such play is praying with the intention of love. Third, spiritual discipline may arise from the fact that one knows that there is nothing else to do except pray. Prayer must not be based on a desire for visions or signs—for proofs which might satisfy an unhealthy curiosity or for a merely speculative knowledge that would do violence to the Divine mystery. But it may properly be rooted in our knowledge of the nature of things, and hence in an awareness of the Absolute and the Infinite. He who really knows that nothing exists except God, and that God is pre-eminently whatever exists, cannot but act consequentially, and this act is Prayer. This may be referred to as the intention of knowledge.

As perhaps you have noticed, these three motives for Prayer—fear, love, and knowledge—correspond respectively to the three faculties of the soul: the will, the sentiment, and the intelligence. We could say, in fact, that the volitive soul, the affective soul, and the cognitive soul each has its own distinctive and intrinsic motive for praying, and together they provide us with fitting and spiritually acceptable reasons for following a spiritual path. Any one of them is enough for the necessary concentration and focus on God. "The man who prays because he really wants to escape hell," or "because he loves God and loves to pray," or "because the reality of God concretely imposes itself on his mind—such a man will realize fervor without difficulty and consequently concentration, singlemindedness, and contemplative inwardness." Every man of course has a soul, and every soul contains all of these faculties. Hence no one's intentions are ever confined to a single plane, to fear or to love or to knowledge alone. The life of Prayer always embraces all three, even as the life of Virtue always includes humility, charity, and veracity. A given man's motive, however, will be predominantly volitive, affective, or intellective depending upon his spiritual type or tendency. This takes us back to the very start of our discussion, where I mentioned the principal human temperaments and the spiritual paths to which they correspond: the way of good works or *karma yoga*, which lays its stress on the will and on the motive of salvation, the way of devotion or *bhakti yoga*, which puts the emphasis on the sentiment and on the motive of love, and the way of gnosis—*jnana yoga*—which speaks primarily to the intelligence and lays its stress on the intention of knowledge.

Ours is the path of *gnosis*, and our intention in Prayer will therefore be based primarily upon our understanding of metaphysical principles. If when we pray we mean to concentrate, to overcome the numerous distractions both without and within, it will be above all through a deliberate recollection of Truth: the Truth about the degrees of Reality, the doctrine of illusion, and the nature of man, and of course the Truth about God. An intention is one's reason for acting, and that act which is Prayer will in our case depend upon a knowledge of transcendence and immanence, a knowledge or *jnana* which inevitably ends up including both *karma* and *bhakti* as well.

For to know that God is completely beyond all that exists is to be filled with a longing for freedom from the world and the ego. True knowledge cannot but make us humble, nor can it fail to crystallize within us the intention of fear. And to know that God is inwardly present at the very heart of whatever exists is to be filled with a profound respect for all things. True knowledge cannot but make us charitable, nor can it fail to kindle within us the intention of love.

✤ Chapter 23 ✤

Invocation of the Name

God and His Name are one.

*P*rayer is our movement toward God, and it brings into play everything which contributes to our finally reaching that goal. It depends upon both our faith and God's grace, and it involves a certain method or discipline which is meant to lead by right intention to unbroken concentration. When we hear the term *prayer*, however, we ordinarily do not think of something quite so large and encompassing. What comes to mind first is simply the act of talking to God. To pray is to make use of words, whether spoken or silent, in addressing ourselves to Heaven.

Prayer in this more specific sense comprises three levels or modes. These are personal or individual Prayer, canonical or liturgical Prayer, and quintessential Prayer, also called Invocation, ejaculatory Prayer, or Prayer of the Heart. Personal Prayer is "the most elementary mode" of contact between man and God. It is the spontaneous and "direct expression of the individual, of his desires and fears, his hopes and gratitude." Its aim is "not only to obtain particular favors," whether for oneself or for others, but also "the purification of the soul: it loosens psychological knots or, in other words, dissolves subconscious coagulations and drains away many secret poisons; it externalizes before God the difficulties, failures, and cris-

169

pations of the soul," and opens it to grace. Especially powerful examples of this first kind of Prayer can be found in the Psalms. Such Prayer includes the expression of "gratitude, resignation, regret, resolution, and praise." Gratitude is "the consciousness that every favor of destiny is a grace which might not have been given." Resignation is "the anticipated acceptance of the nonfulfilment of some request." Regret, contrition, or confession "implies consciousness of what puts us in opposition to the Divine Will." Resolution has to do with "the desire to remedy a given transgression, for our weakness must not make us forget that we are free." Finally, praise "signifies not only that we relate every value to its ultimate Source, but also that we see every trial in terms of its necessity or its usefulness."

The second kind of Prayer, canonical Prayer, is similar to the first in its discursive form and in its use of petitions. But its value in the spiritual life is greater, and this is for two reasons. On the one hand, unlike the spontaneous Prayer of the individual man, "God is its author." It is canonical precisely because it is given to man by God Himself and thus comes with the authority of Revelation. This is the case, for example, with the Lord's Prayer. The superior value of canonical Prayer results on the other hand from the fact that "the reciting subject is not a particular individual, but man as such, the human species." Such Prayer contains petitions that are of concern to everyone, and in this way it includes all possible personal prayers. "Canonical Prayer shows its universality and its timeless value by being very often expressed in the first person plural." It is impossible for whoever recites it not "to pray for all and in all."

Some might object that because it lacks the spontaneity of personal Prayer, canonical Prayer can too easily become mechanical. For this reason it is sometimes thought to lack the value of its individual counterpart. But I am speaking at the moment strictly about the content of Prayer, and from this point of view, the formal prayers enjoined by a revealed tradition are superior to personal petition. "Canonical Prayer expresses fundamental truths and positions which man must necessarily assimilate or realize"—every man, no matter his particular station or needs. This is obviously not the case when we turn to any given individual's personal discourse with God. Of course these fundamental truths must still be assimilated by the individual, and he must therefore make an effort to recite such Prayer with attention and concentration, remembering who it is that he is addressing. After all, "we do not pray in order to perform a traditional and orthodox rite; we pray in order to say something to God."

Third is the highest kind of Prayer, Prayer of the Heart or Invocation. I must pause, however, to guard against a possible misunderstanding. In distinguishing between several levels of Prayer and in ranking their value or efficacy, the spiritual teacher is not suggesting that the "less perfect" modes are therefore useless or unnecessary. On the contrary, all three kinds of Prayer are to be a part of the aspirant's daily spiritual discipline. As we have seen, man embraces multiple levels. On the one hand, he is an individual being in both soul and body, a creature of the Divine Creator. He will therefore have need for addressing God discursively, whether about those things that concern him uniquely or with regard to what he shares with other people. Hence the importance of both personal and canonical Prayer. But on the other hand, by virtue of the Intellect, man also contains a supra-individual and transpersonal dimension. Through this Intellect, he is able to participate in principle in the Divine Essence. In the perspective of *gnosis*, this participation is the ultimate aim of the spiritual life—a participation in fact, and not simply in principle. Our final goal is to share in the inner life of God Himself. If a spiritual practice is going to be an effective means to this end, it must include a mode of Prayer that is more than discursive and petitionary—one which is consistent with the nature of intellection, and one which therefore opens onto the supreme identity of the Self. Here is where Invocation or Prayer of the Heart enters in.

Like the first two modes, Prayer of the Heart also makes use of words. Its value, however, lies not in the discursive meaning that is expressed by those words, not in the propositional significance of certain formulations as such, but in the fact that the words contain a Name of God. An example which may be familiar to you is the Jesus Prayer. The person using this prayer continually repeats the phrase *Lord Jesus Christ, Son of God, have mercy upon me*, or some variation. In reciting these words, he is less concerned with the analytical meaning of the formula than with focusing his attention on the Divine Name of Jesus. The Name is the jewel upon which he concentrates. It is the pearl of great price, and the purpose of the other words of the prayer is to provide it with a suitable setting.

The transformative power of this form of Prayer comes precisely from that Name, and the power of the Name results in turn from the fact that "God and His Name are mysteriously identical." The Name is the uncreated Word or *Logos* in which or through which God utters Himself. For this reason it is really God, not the individual man, who is the subject in this mode of Prayer. "God Himself pronounces His Name in Himself, hence in eternity and outside all creation, so that His unique and uncreate Word is the prototype of ejaculatory Prayer." In this sense, "human invocation is only the 'outward' effect of eternal and 'inward' invocation by the Divinity. The same holds good for every other Revelation: it is sacrificial for the Divine Spirit and liberating for man." The word *Revelation* is very important. The repetitive technique of Invocation as such has no efficacy of its own. In order for an invocatory method to be of spiritual benefit to us, the Name we invoke must be revealed by God and sanctioned by the living tradition which we ourselves follow. There are many false teachers who promote the use of invocations or mantras that are merely human inventions. Sometimes meaningless coinages, often merely banal in their sentiments, these formulas are either useless or dangerous as the case may be, and should be avoided at all costs. "Only that which is given by God has value for salvation, not that which is taken by man; it is God who has revealed His Names, and it is He who determines their usage."

You will recall what we said about Beauty and the symbolism implicit in the nature of things. Like all forms of Beauty, the Name is a link to Heaven. But where Beauty corresponds metaphysically to the Manifestation of the Principle, the Name is the very Principle in Manifestation, and through it "there takes place the mysterious meeting of the created and the Uncreate, the contingent and the Absolute, the finite and the Infinite." The Name, one might say, is a sacrament. It is the outward and visible sign of an inward and spiritual grace, although the term *grace* may not be strong enough in this case. Like the sacrament of the Eucharist, the Name communicates to the one who invokes it the Real Presence of God Himself. It is for this reason that the masters of the spiritual life surround the practice of Invocation with many of the same precautions and safeguards that are reserved by theologians for Holy Communion. "If, according to the Apostle, 'whosoever shall eat this bread unworthily eateth damnation to himself,' the same holds true for the presumptuous use of ejaculatory prayers." To invoke the Name of God is to enter into the very presence of God, or to call that Presence into oneself. "By the Name, the Named makes Himself present." To practice

Prayer of the Heart is "to offer the space of our soul to the Divine Presence, by means precisely of the Name of God: to allow God to enter our space, in order that God may allow us to enter His space."

We have said that the Name is a liberation for man. "Quintessential Prayer brings about an escape from the world and from life, and thereby confers a new and Divine sap upon the veil of appearances and the current of forms, and a fresh meaning to our presence amid the play of phenomena." I can perhaps best explain what this means by reminding you once more of the law of inverse analogy. What is low in the Principle is high in Manifestation, and what is outward in Heaven is inward on earth. The Divine Name represents for God a determination or limitation at the level of the relative Absolute or Being, and it is through this determination that the world is created. But from man's point of view within the world, this same Name is a means of exit or liberation from the conditions of existence. It is the place where Manifestation opens onto the Principle. "God, in naming Himself, firstly determines Himself as Being and secondly, starting from Being, manifests Himself as Creation." On the other hand, "man, for his part, when pronouncing the same Name, describes the inverse movement, for this Name is not only Being and Creation, but also Mercy and Redemption; in man, it does not create, but on the contrary 'undoes,' and that in a Divine manner since it brings man back to the Principle." Speaking alchemically, we could say that what is coagulation in Heaven is solution on earth. Since God created the world by His Name, man may return to God by the same means. "There is direct analogy in the sense that man, like God, pronounces the Name, and inverse analogy in the sense that man, by invoking, annihilates—for himself—this world, while God creates it." The annihilation is no outward destruction, of course. In fact, from a different angle, the practice of Invocation has the effect of restoring our lost vision of the goodness and the splendor of creatures. "Things become transparent and transmit to us rays of their immutable and blessed archetypes." The annihilation or extinction is of a metaphysical order, corresponding to our awareness of the relativity of the world. "The sufficient reason for the Invocation of the Name is the remembering of God; and this, in the final analysis, is not other than consciousness of the Absolute. The Name actualizes this consciousness and, in the end, perpetuates it in the soul and fixes it in the heart, so that it penetrates the whole being and at the same time transmutes and absorbs it."

If Prayer is the essence of the spiritual life, then Invocation is the essence of Prayer. It is therefore to be stressed more than any other spiritual practice. Everything else has been a prelude to this. Truth, Virtue, and Beauty were preparations for Prayer, and so also have our discussions of meditation, concentration, and intention been preparations for invoking the Name. I have several times spoken about the importance of becoming focused on God, and you may well have wondered just how this was to be done. Once we have established a space for our Prayer and put aside the demands of time, what exactly are we supposed to do? Once we have formed a proper intention and are able to concentrate, upon what are we supposed to concentrate? The answer in both cases is provided by Prayer of the Heart. What you are to do is invoke, and it is upon the Divine Name which you invoke that you concentrate. It is not enough simply to tell ourselves not to think about the world and to think instead about God. A central support for attention is necessary, or we shall otherwise suffer from an endless succession of speculations. "One can meditate or speculate indefinitely on transcendent truths and their applications." Indeed we could "spend a whole lifetime speculating on the supra-sensorial and the transcendent." But what really matters in the final analysis is "the fixation of spirit and soul in an unthinkable dimension of the Real." Here is the value of a revealed Name of God. The Name is a center, a focus, a support, and the proper basis for this crystallization of spirit and soul. It must become our life.

The efficacy of the practice flows in part from its very simplicity. In fact, all of the many complexities and numerous distinctions of metaphysical doctrine can be reduced to the unity of the Name alone. The way of knowledge is entirely implicit within it. "If there were no points at which the incommensurable complexity of the Real became quite simple, quite tangible, we would have no possibility of contact with Truth." The Name, however, is simplicity itself, and its pronunciation is the most direct of all possible contacts and the most tangible of acts. Because of its power and profundity, it is well suited to being the central discipline of our formal retreats. And yet because of its simplicity, it can also be easily used at other times as a continual, and in principle perpetual, reminder of God. For the practice of Invocation "can be superimposed on any legitimate action," and though it "cannot be superimposed on every beautiful or useful thought," it can "continue to vibrate during the course of such a thought." Our thinking or "mental articulation, although in practice excluding Prayer—to the extent that the mind cannot do two things at once—nevertheless does not interrupt the 'remembrance' in the eyes of God." Careful attention to the essentials of Virtue and Beauty provides a fitting context or ambience for invoking the Name. But at the same time, the Name itself has the power to create its own space, and since it may be pronounced in every setting and on every occasion, it has the capacity to turn every moment into a spiritual retreat.

A word of caution, however. The simplicity of the Invocation must not tempt you to any lack of intensity. One can call upon God with the lighthearted freedom of the child, but not with impudence or lack of reverence. For though it is simple, the Name is also holy. And while the Invocation can be practiced with ease, it must still be practiced, and this means effort and discipline, which are not always easy. "In the spiritual life, the difficulties often lie in apparently easy things; victory is his who, in secret, knows how to persevere in little things," for "there are things that are little in themselves, but which practiced with perseverance entail great things." In any case, if you wish to practice the Invocation, you must first understand how very serious a matter it is. The Name is no plaything, and Invocation is not recreation. Those who would enter upon the way of the Name should realize that it will demand all that they are. "God and His Name are one," and it is in the nature of things that the sovereignty of God should require the totality of man. He who aspires to this practice should therefore begin only after having first vowed to continue to the very end of his life.

The aspirant must "enter into a concrete and solemn engagement," and "this engagement is irreversible: the way is one of no return."

❖ Chapter 24 ❖

Spiritual Direction

A spiritual means has significance only within the rules assigned to it by the tradition which offers it, whether it is a question of outward or inward rules; nothing is more dangerous than to give oneself up to improvisations in this field.

*W*ith our discussion of the Name, we have come at last to the most important practice in the spiritual life, and the one which our authorities tell us is best suited to the present age. But we have also reached a point where I must lay down some warnings.

I ended the last chapter by explaining that the Invocation is a spiritual method which should be practiced only on condition that one is fully aware of its solemnity, profundity, and holiness. All Prayer presupposes a foundation in Truth and a context made possible by Virtue and Beauty, and so also for Prayer of the Heart. And yet this highest mode of Prayer is unique in having God Himself as its content. For this reason it must be approached with a preparation that is all the more strict and exacting. One may be readily attracted by the directness and simplicity of the practice, but this should be balanced by a sober respect for its power—a power, we are told, which can prove too much for those who are not qualified or who attempt to make use of the method for the wrong reasons or without the necessary protection. There is actually something

177

rather disproportionate or anomalous in my even mentioning such a practice in a public setting like this. In former times, instruction in these matters would have been strictly oral, and reserved for those who had proven themselves worthy. I would therefore "doubtless hesitate to speak of these things if others did not speak of them, and if we were not living at a time when all sorts of testimonies are demanded and when the compensating Mercy simplifies many things." In any case, "it is better that wisdom should be divulged than that it should be forgotten." In an age of confusion and thirst, when seekers like you are otherwise likely to be led astray by numerous errors, "the advantages of communication are greater than those of secrecy."

Nevertheless, it is the responsibility of those who assist in this communication to make sure that the unprecedented accessibility of spiritual teachings today does not lead to a last state that is worse than the first. When it comes to the Name, this means stressing that no one should presume to engage in the practice of methodic Invocation on his own. Here the advice that you have asked for is more than advice. I am not simply suggesting or recommending something. I am insisting as strongly as I possibly can that if you aspire to invoking the Name, you should not even consider trying to do so by yourself. Whether or not you follow the invocatory way is a matter which you are obviously free to decide for yourself, within the framework of what destiny permits. But once you have elected to pursue such a path, you will have to put aside any desire you may have had to do things on your own initiative or in your own way. Personal and canonical prayers are one thing. Every man may, and should, make them a part of his daily life. But quintessential Prayer of the Heart is something different, and for this you need help.

Two things are necessary. First, you must have a sacramental affiliation with a living tradition, and second, you must be under the guidance of a spiritual director. We have said that metaphysics, morality, aesthetics, and method are indispensable to the spiritual journey. But orthodoxy and authority are indispensable, too. Provision is made for them precisely by our initiation into a revealed tradition and by our submission to the direction of a qualified guide. Each of these elements, I might add, confirms the other. If you are in doubt as to which way to turn, it will be helpful to know that no valid tradition would ever deny the importance of spiritual direction. Similarly, there is no legitimate teacher or director who would ever question the importance of an orthodox affiliation. Being aware of this reciprocity can be of great assistance when we must distinguish the true from the false.

First, tradition. "In order to activate intellectual 'reminiscence,' man, who bears the mark of the fall, needs to proceed circuitously and to come to the inward by way of the outward." By the outward is meant here the forms—the scriptures, the dogmas, the moral precepts, the rituals, the symbols—of a given religion. The authentic esoterist is the first to insist on the value of these exoteric elements, for he knows that the kernel requires the protection of its shell, and that "a spirituality deprived of these bases can only end up as a psychological exploit without any relation to the unfolding of our higher states." Of course, the forms in question must be genuine expressions of Truth, and they must therefore be rooted in authentic Revelation. As you will perhaps remember from the Introduction, the term *tradition*, as used here, has to do with the reverberation through time of an entry by God into space. I used the image of waves in a pool radiating out from the central impact of a descending stone. Where Revelation corresponds to a vertical descent of the Truth, tradition refers to its horizontal extension. In any case, we are told that "although intellection can occur, as an isolated miracle, wherever the intellective faculty exists," nevertheless "an intellection outside tradition," and therefore independent of the grace of Heaven, "will have neither authority nor efficacy." On the contrary, "intelligence and metaphysical certainty alone do not save, and do not of themselves prevent titanic falls."

Why is this so? The answer in part is that an authentic tradition speaks to the whole of man, to the spirit and the soul and the body. By bringing all of these levels of the microcosm into play—by providing doctrine for the mind, moral precepts for the will, objects of devotion for the sentiment, and ritual for the body—it serves to protect us against the hypertrophy or deviation of any one of these levels. And yet this is to touch only the surface. We are dealing with imponderables here. There is no way to catalogue the full benefits of a tradition in advance of attaching yourself to it, nor to explain to the skeptical mind how exactly a religion protects us. This seems to be a case once again where the proof comes only in the practice, only through experiencing in particular the sacramental grace of initiation.

My emphasis on the importance of undertaking the spiritual journey within the framework of a living tradition will prove an obstacle
for many who might otherwise find themselves attracted to the perspective of *gnosis*. I am accustomed to people protesting that this is
a kind of fundamentalism or narrowmindedness on the part of our
traditionalist teachers. They seem to suppose that newer means better with regard to spiritual methods—that the latest concoction of
some enterprising and self-acclaimed guru, who purports to be more
closely attuned to the expectations of modern man, is superior to traditions that are centuries old, and which continue to bear the fruit of
great saints. The assumption appears to be that "'religion is made for
man,' and that it must therefore adapt itself to his needs," and that
through their failure to do so, the ancient spiritual patrimonies of
mankind have "become bankrupt." One might as well say, however,
that "the alphabet has become bankrupt in a class where the pupils
are determined not to learn it," where a continued spiritual illiteracy
is preferred because of the convenient excuse it provides for the ego's
laziness and pride. Whatever the reasons a man might give for dis-
missing tradition, the insistence on a traditional religious affiliation
is in the final analysis for his own practical good, and not out of some
nostalgic allegiance to the past. Not of course that salvation is
impossible otherwise. God remains quite capable of delivering a soul
which through no fault of its own has been deprived of contact with
a traditional spiritual authority. The Divine Spirit blows where it
wills. Nevertheless from our side, only an immense pride and ingrat-
itude, as well as the lack of all sense of proportion, could lead a man
to prefer his own lights to the proven efficacy of the immeasurable
gifts of Divine Revelation. If you are serious about the spiritual life,
you simply must take the necessary steps to enter upon an orthodox
tradition.

A traditional affiliation, however, is not itself enough for those
wishing to undertake a practice like the Invocation. It is also essential that they place themselves under the guidance of a spiritual
director. This is going to be a hard saying for some, for the idea of
submitting oneself to the guidance of another human being is one
which flatly contradicts the individualism that most of us have been
taught to hold sacred. It is a requirement which will perhaps be
especially distasteful to "those who hold that man is free in all
respects before God, and who will ask by what right we seek to subject Prayer to conditions." In the case of the Invocation, however, "the

reply is simple, and it is the Bible itself which gives it: 'Thou shalt not take the Name of the Lord thy God in vain.'" The ultimate aim of our practice is to escape from the tyranny of the ego, but there could be no greater vanity than supposing liberation to be possible on the ego's own terms. This is why it is said that the man who chooses himself for a master has chosen a fool, and this is the reason that direction by another person is so important.

Spiritual direction is critical for at least two reasons. It is important first of all at the start of the path because of the delicate and very exacting conditions and qualifications which the use of the Name presupposes. "Being founded on pure intellection on the one hand and on a subtle and rigorous technique on the other, and bringing into play both the constitution of the microcosm and universal analogies," Prayer of the Heart depends upon "an intellectual preparation and a psychological conditioning anchored in the tradition," not in a profane modern environment. Apart from a firm foundation in Truth, Virtue, and Beauty, such a method cannot but "remain ineffective, or still worse lead in the opposite direction." This is the mistake committed by the proponents of the many new age movements of our day, "who believe that they must offer to the least apt and the least informed people a 'purely scientific' and 'non-sectarian' way," one which they claim is "freed from all superstition," but which in reality is "freed from all traditional safeguards and indeed from every adequate reason for existing." A spiritual director who is himself leading the life of a living tradition plays a double role. On the one hand, he protects the Name from profanation, and on the other hand, he protects the aspirant who might otherwise find himself playing with fire. The guide fulfills these twin functions by explaining the necessary requirements of the way and by evaluating the seeker's qualifications to meet them. If the spiritual journey consists in becoming what one is, spiritual qualification consists in being what one is to become, and only the experienced guide is capable of discerning whether a given aspirant meets this condition.

Direction is also crucial as we advance in the way. The practice of quintessential Prayer "imposes on the soul an immense disproportion owing to the fact that it introduces the presence of the sacred into the darkness of human imperfection," and "this inevitably provokes disequilibrium-producing reactions, which in principle carry with them the risk of an irremediable fall." The presence of the Name means death to the ego, and the ego will therefore do everything in its power either to avoid the Name altogether or, what is worse, to appropriate the Invocation as an instrument for achieving its own purposes and fulfilling its own desires. The results of this misuse of the sacred may include bouts of depression, unexpected psychic powers, and other demonic distractions and unusual experiences that we are not ourselves capable of situating or handling. "Every spiritual alchemy involves an anticipated death and consequently also certain losses of equilibrium or periods of obscuration." In following the path, a man eventually comes to a point where "he is no longer completely of this world, nor yet of the other, and his experience seems to call into question all the existential categories of which we are so to speak woven. In these 'trials' and in the 'temptations' which accompany them," the spiritual director is a source of stability and a "'motionless center.' To the temptation of giving rational form to irrational troubles, he opposes objective, immutable, and incorruptible Truth. The same is true with regard to temptations of the opposite kind, when the disciple, submerged by some contemplative state beyond his usual reach (and such a state may only be accidental and is not proof of realization), may think that to some degree he has become superhuman." It is doubtless the case that "grace surrounds us infinitely, and it is only our hardness that makes us impervious to its radiation." It is also true that "accidental fissures" may occur in this egoistic carapace, with the result that "the soul finds itself enraptured by the irradiations of pre-existing grace." But such experiences must not be allowed to deflect us from the one thing needful, which is concentration by right intention on the Name alone. The director is there in part to provide us with essential reminders as to what is really important.

I should explain that when I speak of directors, I have in mind two kinds. On the one hand, there is the spiritual master. This is the man who has already realized the final goal of the way, one in whom the ego has been permanently extinguished, and in whom the Intellect has fully penetrated both the soul and the body. He knows that which is because he is that which knows, and his very person has thus become a teaching. There are undoubtedly degrees or stations among such masters as well as hierarchical differences in scope and function. But these will be more or less invisible from the point of view of the seeker. What counts is the fact that "every spiritual master, by his knowledge and his function and by the graces attaching to them, is mysteriously assimilated to his prototypes"—that is, to his predecessors in the spiritual way and ultimately, through them, to the Heaven-sent founder of the tradition which he represents. In placing oneself under the direction of such a man, one is placing oneself at the disposal of the Divine Spirit itself.

Such a teacher, of course, is quite rare. Very few of us will ever have the opportunity to meet a true master. You need not despair, however, for there is also the man whom we may call an instructor. This is someone who has experience in the spiritual life, who is further advanced than we are, and who can transmit to us all the necessary information. The wise counsel and spiritual friendship of such a person is extremely valuable. Besides being able to explain the rules of Prayer and to instruct us in certain basic techniques, he provides if nothing else a kind of second opinion. On the principle that two heads are better than one, he helps us avoid being swallowed up by our ego's pretentions. Having recourse to an instructor, we are told, "is not ideal." It would doubtless be better if every seeker had the personal guidance of a master. But for most of us this is simply impossible "in the actual world." We may be grateful instead for the encouragement of a more experienced fellow traveler.

You should understand, however, that unlike a master, an instructor cannot of his own authority confer upon us the right to practice the quintessential Prayer of Invocation. Nor should we presume to seize this right for ourselves. If we wish for the great privilege of invoking the Name, we shall need to look directly to Heaven. The Christian, for example, will turn quite naturally to Christ and the Virgin while others will petition elsewhere. But petition we must, for "it is impossible to approach God, or the Absolute, or the Self, without the blessing and aid of Heaven." In the absence of a master's initiatic benediction, it is especially important that your prayers be accompanied by a sacred vow signifying your commitment for life. As we have remarked before, the way is one of no return, and our entry upon it must be marked by due solemnity. It should also be emphasized that even in such a case as I am describing now, the need for spiritual direction is never set aside. Grace will certainly be granted to those who sincerely seek it, but the actual practice of Invocation is to be undertaken even so only with the knowledge and advice of an instructor, and not on one's own independent initiative.

Whether it is a master or an instructor, living contact with another human being who can guide us and help us is absolutely essential in the way of the Name. This leads to a final word of caution. Whatever you do, please do not think that a book can play the role of director. This is a very common temptation, and one into which I have perhaps myself led you by writing down the advice you requested. You need to understand, however, that not even a sacred text like the Bible, let alone a mere book of advice, can perform the indispensable function of guide. Unlike people, books are not able to correct us when we misinterpret them. Moreover, by introducing "a quasi-absolute element of conclusiveness, and thus of petrification and sterility, into the very expression of Truth," a written text, appearing after all so solid and fixed, may give us the quite mistaken impression that we know a great deal more than we actually do. Nor can a book, by its very nature, protect us from depending too much on the mind, from our tendency to confine the Truth to a merely mental plane. As long as we are reading, we cannot stop thinking, and yet progress in the spiritual life requires that at certain points we do stop thinking so that the ideas we have begun learning can start to penetrate the rest of our being. The spiritual seeker "needs light, but he also needs an element of obscurity which will act as a leaven with respect to the light received, and which will help him to release the element of light which he carries in his own substance." Books can shed light, and they can stimulate thought, but unlike a living guide, who can teach us by his very actions and presence and silence, they can also get in the way of our fully responding to that light. I do not know about you, but I for one am very pleased that this particular book has nearly reached its conclusion. It is time to do something about all these words. It is time for Prayer.

"There is analysis, and there is synthesis. Sometimes it is necessary to make difficult, and other times it is necessary to simplify; it is necessary sometimes to learn, and sometimes to forget. We will even say that in the spiritual life, it is sometimes necessary to forget so that the thing learned may be able to bear its fruit; for the 'seed cannot sprout if the grain doth not die.'"

Chapter 25

Our Final Goal

Man stands in front of a mountain which he must remove with his own hands. He digs away the earth, but in vain; the mountain remains. Man however goes on digging, in the Name of God. And the mountain vanishes. It was never there.

*B*efore we conclude, a few words should be added about the end of our way. I realize that this may appear premature. Although our discussion of spirituality is about to come to a close, the journey itself is only beginning. As I have insisted repeatedly, advice is one thing, and putting it into practice is another. It may therefore seem too soon to anticipate the full fruits of that practice.

No doubt the serious seeker must avoid jumping to conclusions. In fact, about the worst mistake he could make would be to suppose that metaphysical and esoteric descriptions of the supreme human state can be personally appropriated by those who are just setting out on the path. It is true that "the man who is undelivered is in reality a delivered man ignorant of himself," and true as well that we must become what we are. But we must not take such maxims as grounds for compounding our problems by forgetting the ignorance and neglecting the real work of becoming. Above all, "one must take care not to transfer the voluntaristic and sentimental

185

individualism of religious zeal onto the plane of transpersonal awareness," for "it is not we who know God; it is God who knows Himself in us."

Nonetheless, if we are cautious as to how we use them, anticipations of our final goal can be of great help in our journey toward it. If the seeker's efforts and energies are to be expended properly and efficiently, it is important that they be given direction. The archer needs a target at which to aim. This target, however, must be proportionate to the nature of things, in this case to the nature of man himself. It must not be set up at a distance which will tempt us to overshoot our proper mark, but neither should it be positioned in such a way that we fail to live up to our full potential. Presumption and laziness must both be discouraged.

As usual, the *jnani* or gnostic pursues a middle way. On the one hand, he means to go far beyond the merely political goals of those who seek only a social or economic liberation, and who under cover of what they call charity would dissuade us from aspiring to anything more than a secular utopia. But on the other hand, authentic *gnosis* stops well short of the Prometheanism implicit in so much of what passes for esoterism today. To all those blind guides who neglect the essential distinction between the individual levels of our being and the transpersonal Intellect, who act as if a man's aim is to become his own god, the perennial philosopher consistently responds with an insistence on grace and the virtues, especially humility, and he issues a warning that "union is not for the ego." The proper end of man is far more than a worldly well-being or mere social justice, more even than the blissful rewards of Paradise envisaged by the *bhakta*. But at the same time, it is an end which in no way compromises the supremacy and sovereignty of God, who remains for all eternity our Creator and Lord.

How then should we picture the end of the journey? What are we aiming at? What is our final goal? The goal can be stated both positively and negatively. It is an attainment, but it is also an escape or liberation.

To put the matter first in its positive form, our highest calling "is to realize that which is man's reason for being." The esoterist continues to direct our attention to the clues inscribed in the very substance of our nature. I am to become what I am. I am to realize the true significance of the human possibility. And this means fulfilling my vocation as "a projection of God and therefore a bridge between earth and Heaven." Man is a microcosm, but for that reason he is also a pontifex. The degrees of Reality are all present within him, and therein they find their true connection. All things of course are Divine projections in some sense, for all Manifestation is of the Principle. But unlike the other creatures of his universe, man can become aware of this metaphysical Truth, and to the extent he is aware, he becomes a conscious participant in the process of the projection itself. This participation, by virtue of the Intellect, results in "a point of view that allows God to see Himself starting from an other-than-Himself, even though this other, in the final analysis, can only be Himself." Man is meant to be a mode of God's knowledge of God, and the goal of our path is that this purpose might be fulfilled.

To express the same point negatively, we could say that "the path is the passage from potentiality to virtuality, and from virtuality to actuality, its summit being the state of the one 'delivered in this life'"—in Hindu terms, "the *jivan-mukta*." This deliverance is a liberation in part from passions and pride. Our constant aim should be "the cessation of egoity," a permanent detachment from the "phenomenal nucleus which is the empirical ego." The end of the journey is the "sleep" of this ego and "the wake of the immortal soul—of the ego fed on sensorial impressions and filled with desires, and of the soul, free and crystallized in God." We are told that "the moving surface of our being must sleep and must therefore withdraw from images and instincts, whereas the depths of our being must be awake in the consciousness of the Divine, thus illuminating, like a motionless flame, the silence of the holy sleep." The empirical ego is sometimes compared to "a watermill whose wheel, under the drive of a current—the world and life—turns and repeats itself untiringly, in a series of images always different and always similar." We shall have reached the conclusion of our journey when the movement of this wheel has once and for all come to a stop.

If we are to understand our final goal, it is necessary that we return one last time to a consideration of the Absolute and the Infinite. We have learned that God is utterly beyond everything else, ourselves included, and that in comparison with Him, we are as nothing. The Divine Reality is transcendent unicity. And yet because He exceeds all things, no limits can be placed upon God. Nothing can exclude or resist Him. As a result He is everywhere, such that all things, ourselves included, are fundamentally or essentially nothing other than God. The Divine Reality is immanent totality. An adequate eschatology, or doctrine of last things, must be faithful as always to these two fundamental truths. It must insist, on the one hand, that no matter how high man might ascend, he can never equal God, nor could he ascend or advance at all were it not for the grace which lends him at every moment the dignity of existence itself. "Man as such cannot bring an activity to bear upon God, who alone is pure Act. The creature is always passive in relation to the Creator and His graces." On the other hand—from another, equally legitimate angle—even though man may seem outwardly a virtual nothing, inwardly and essentially he is not other than God, for strictly speaking, there is nothing other to be. Our aim is to realize our identity with the Divine Self, which is "the absolute, unique, and immanent Subject of our subjectivity." The way of knowledge can have no less a goal. For "he who says 'to know' says 'to know that which is,'" and "he who says 'to know that which is' says, in the final analysis, 'to be that which knows': the Self."

The esoterist guards this crucial paradox by distinguishing between two selves or *I*'s in man, between two levels or degrees in God, and between two different axes of relationship between man and God. You are familiar with the first and second of these distinctions. In the first place, "it is necessary to know that in man there is, in principle, a double subjectivity." There is the subjectivity or self of the empirical ego, which falsely supposes itself a true *I* while in fact it is but the conditioned effect of relative and transient forces. And there is the Intellect, which lies beyond the domain of individual existence. The property and possession of no man, the Intellect lies at the very root of our knowledge. As for the distinction of levels in God, this brings us back to the difference between the Absolute as such, or Beyond-Being, and the relative Absolute, or Being. The former, as you will remember, is the Divine Essence, while the latter is the Divine Person.

The axes of relationship between man and God are the connections which exist, at least in principle, between the ego and the Divine Person, on the one hand, and between the Intellect and the Divine Essence, on the other. The perennial philosophy cautions us to make certain that these two relationships are not confused. Their "erroneous mixture" in "partial or imperfectly elucidated esoterisms" is precisely what leads to the "metaphysical individualism" of those who forget, or rather ignore, the fact that "the ego as such cannot logically seek the experience of what lies beyond egoity," and who therefore end up promoting the absurd and very dangerous idea that the individual human being can become a kind of deity.

The relationship of the ego to God is always with God as Person, and it must remain one of submission and faith. God is the Lord of the human individual. The individual in turn is His creature and servant. No matter the degree of our spiritual attainment, "the servant cannot change into the Lord." Nevertheless there is at the same time "something in the servant that is capable—though not without the Lord's grace—of surpassing the axis 'servant-Lord' or 'subject-object' and of realizing the absolute 'Self.'" This something is the Intellect, through which a man may come to participate in the very Essence of God. "God shows Himself as creative Person insofar as—or in relation to the fact that—we are 'creature' and individual, but that particular reciprocal relationship is far from exhausting all our ontological and intellectual nature." We are more than individuals. We are inwardly an openness onto the Infinite. There is "verticality in the face of 'our Father who art in Heaven.'" But there must also be "inwardness in virtue of the 'Kingdom of God which is within you.'"

I have said that the Intellect is the name for this openness or inwardness. The Intellect is only "a mirror," however. Even in the man who possesses it in fact and not merely in principle, it "must not be confused with spiritual realization." Realization means that "our being, and not merely our thought, participates in the objects which the mirror reflects." This is why intellection must be joined with Virtue and Prayer if we are to grasp, and then become, what we see. And yet even then it is not really we who become it. God alone can know God, and at the moment of realization, His knowledge is no more and no less than what it always was, though now it is within us, and we are in it.

Please remember that all these distinctions are finally just symbols of what cannot be said, dialectical strategems designed to aid us in thinking the unthinkable. I do not want you to go away supposing that God is somehow composed of parts, that there is something called the Divine Being or Person and some other separate thing that we are obliged to refer to as Beyond-Being or Essence. "Being does not divide God," for in fact "it does not leave the pure Essence." The Divine Person of the Creator and Lord "is not like one half of a circle which is divided in two; it is like the circumference surrounding the center." Nor is man divided. Ego and Intellect are aspects of a single human nature. "The ego itself, considered as the subjective

kernel or 'heart' of the individuality, is an 'inward outwardness' insofar as it is hardened and consequently immersed in the world"—to
the extent, in other words, that it gives rise to such and such an ego.
But this same ego as such, understood as the very principle of our
individuality, "becomes an 'outward inwardness' if it softens in
response to the attraction of the Divine Center and plunges its roots
therein." There is finally but one human *I*, and this *I* or ego is simultaneously a reflection and a negation of the supreme Self. "God can
consequently be called the 'Divine I' by analogy with what is positive,
conscious, and immortal in the human 'I,'" for there is only one Self,
and insofar as I am truly myself, and not a mere bundle of reactions
and memories, I cannot but be one with that Self. But on the other
hand, God "can also be called 'He' in opposition to the negative, ignorant, and unreal aspects of the human 'I.'" What I ordinarily call
myself is but a collection of impressions and passions, and to the
extent that these worldly integuments continue to be determinative
factors in my seeming *I*, God is to be regarded as the transcendent
Other. He is my sovereign Lord, and to Him I must give total obedience in faith. Only in this way shall I extinguish all those competing
selves that wish to go by His Name, and only thus shall I become
able to say truly of the immanent Self that *I am*. "The circle of knowledge closes in our personality, in its death in God and in its life in
God." In the final analysis, God is one, and man is one, and there is
but one relationship between them. This relationship in its turn is
one of identity, for ultimately there can be only one *One*.

As we journey toward a realization of this supreme identity, however, neither our discernment that there is nothing but God the
Absolute nor our recognition that everything is God the Infinite
should be allowed to blind us to the greatest mystery of all: the presence of something else, something in the middle, which is neither
nothing nor God and neither ego nor Intellect. This something, of
course, is what we are. It is man. Caught in this middle, provided by
grace with an existence between, we are presented at every moment
of life with a choice: whether to ascend into God or to go down into
nothingness. I began our discussion, in the very first chapter of this
book, by speaking of choice, and I shall have failed you completely if
in closing I neglect to stress one final time how critical this choice
really is. If you are indeed a serious seeker, you will take this emphasis very seriously, and you will not permit all our talk about the

splendor of the prize to eclipse the importance of actually running the race.

"There is in every man an incorruptible star, a substance called upon to become crystallized in Immortality." This Divine calling must be heeded, however, for a vocation is no guarantee of fulfillment. There is indeed an essential identity between man and God, as there is between God and everything else which exists. But this important esoteric Truth must not cause us to overlook the fact that while Reality is one in itself, in Manifestation it is a thing of degrees. Nor dare we forget that on the level at which we exist at the moment, we are faced with an urgent necessity to do all in our power to live up to the precious opportunity that is ours as human beings. For make no mistake: we may well be lost. The metaphysician is no universalist with respect to salvation. He insists on the contrary that damnation is a very real possibility. It is "the reply to the periphery which makes itself the Center"—"the reply of Reality to the ego wanting to be absolute, and condemned to be so without being able to be so." Indeed "the notion of hell becomes perfectly clear when we think how senseless it is—and what a waste and a suicide—to slip through the human state without being truly man: that is, to pass God by, and thus to pass our own souls by, as if we had any right to human faculties," to our intelligence, our will, and our sentiment, "apart from the return to God."

Practically speaking, Prayer is the most important thing in life. Truth, Virtue, and Beauty are ultimately all for its sake. Its importance consists above all in bringing together those "two moments in life which are everything": "the present moment, when we are free to choose what we would be, and the moment of death, when we have no longer any choice and the decision belongs to God." Everything reduces finally to what you are doing right now. "If the present moment is good, death will be good; if we are now with God—in this present moment which is ceaselessly being renewed but which remains this one and only moment of actuality—God will be with us at the moment of death." Being present with God in our prayers "is a death in life; it will be a life in death."

The present moment, death, the encounter with God, then eternity: "all these realities are already present in Prayer, in the timeless actuality of the Divine Presence."

Epilogue:
Perennial Philosophy and
Transcendent Unity

*A*s I explained in the Introduction, the teaching of Frithjof Schuon is at once metaphysical, esoteric, traditional, and perennial. The meditations which followed were concerned primarily with elaborating the first two of those descriptive terms. *Gnosis* is metaphysical, we said, insofar as God the Absolute is beyond all forms and limitation, but it is equally esoteric insofar as God the Infinite is yet within those forms. We also touched briefly on the third of these adjectives, on the traditional dimension of this perspective, notably in our discussion of Prayer, where I stressed the importance of a sacramental affiliation with a revealed religion. "Apprehension of the Truth is possible," we are told, "only on the foundations, and within the framework, willed by God," for our liberation from the ego and the world can take place only by means of what enters into that world from above, and not by the necessarily individual initiatives of the ego itself.

I have not yet discussed, however, what is probably the best known aspect of Schuon's work: his teaching that God has revealed Himself in each of the orthodox religions, and that union with the Divine Reality is therefore possible on the basis of any one of these several traditions. This "universalist" or perennialist dimension is summed up in the assertion that there is a "transcendent unity of religions," and it is to this idea that I would like to turn now. You will understand that I cannot at this point provide anything even close to a full exposition, but perhaps I can at least help to counter some common misunderstandings.

First, a clarification as to the role of religious tradition. As you know, my aim in these pages has been to explain the essential elements of the spiritual life, to take you as directly as possible to the very heart of that life, and this has meant focusing on "the nature of things as perceived by intellectual intuition." We have had in view "not traditional information pure and simple so much as intrinsic doctrinal explanations; that is to say, the expression of truths of which the traditional dialectics are the vestitures." It is therefore not as a historian of ideas or philosopher of comparative religion that I have been writing, nor as a theologian or religious apologist, but strictly as "a spokesman of the *philosophia perennis*," as one who is interested in "the Truth that is everywhere and always the same." No doubt this procedure will have failed to meet the academic expectations of our day, most scholars having been conditioned to suppose that all Truth is conditioned. But it has not been for them that I have offered advice.

I need to make sure, however, that no one—whether scholar or seeker—is left with the impression that the perennial philosophy is some kind of substitute for a revealed tradition, or that metaphysics and esoterism are the same as religion. Although I have approached your question strictly from the point of view of the Intellect, one must never forget that there is more to the human being than intellection alone. "If every man possessed Intellect, not merely in a fragmentary or virtual state, but as a fully developed faculty," then there would be no need for Revelation, since "total intellection would be a natural thing." The problem, however, is the fall. While the "total Truth is inscribed, in an immortal script, in the very substance of our spirit," we are now cut off from that substance, cut off from the Self, and cannot re-enter our center save with the aid of grace—the grace that flows through those objective manifestations of the Divine *Logos* which are the revealed religions. "The Intellect contains in its substance all that is true," but this Truth cannot be fully known, much less fully realized, unless "the Intellect is deployed in the atmosphere of a Revelation." For Revelation is to the macrocosm or human collectivity what intellection is to the microcosm or individual. "What the different Revelations do is to 'crystallize' and 'actualize,' in different degrees according to the case, a nucleus of certitudes which not only abides forever in the Divine Omniscience, but also sleeps by refraction in the 'naturally supernatural' kernel of the individual," that kernel precisely which is the Intellect.

It follows that each of us must be living the life prescribed by a religious tradition if we wish to find our way back to that inwardness where man and God are but one. "In normal conditions," that is, before the advent of the modern, secular world, there would have been no question as to the necessity of such a life, and we would have learned "*a priori* the reality of Divine things through Revelation." Only "*a posteriori*" and as a matter of consequence would the man of a gnostic temperament have had access "to the truth of these things through intellection, which reveals to us their essence lying beyond received formulations." Owing to the skepticism and general loss of faith in the modern world, however, one is often obliged to proceed in reverse and go straight to this essence, since "only esoterism" can "restore the lost truth by referring to the total Truth." And yet this does not mean that Revelation is no longer necessary. Although "the spiritual chaos of our epoch permits or requires that the 'inward' be manifested 'outwardly,'" this is no reason to think that the inward alone can take the place of the outward. The dogmas, the moral code, and above all the sacramental rites of an orthodox tradition are essential provisions for everyone making the spiritual journey.

This of course cannot be proven, any more than a man can see or hear or taste for someone else. As we have noted many times, the proof of such things is in the life. Nor is it possible to provide a detailed catalogue of what you should look for when it comes to finding a truly orthodox way. I would simply observe that the essential elements of spirituality which we have been discussing throughout are at the same time the essential criteria for testing the spirits. There is no such thing as a valid tradition which is lacking in Truth or in Virtue, in Beauty or Prayer. In the first place, "for a religion to be considered as intrinsically orthodox, it must be founded upon a fully adequate doctrine of the Absolute." This point pertains to the ingredient of Truth, for orthodoxy is "not mere fidelity to a system." To be orthodox means "to participate, by way of a doctrine that can properly be called 'traditional,' in the immutability of the principles which govern the Universe and fashion our intelligence." Orthodox dogmas are fundamentally descriptions of the nature of things. But in addition to true doctrine or theory, a valid tradition must also make provision for an effective method or practice. A religion is orthodox on condition that it offers not just "a sufficient, if not always exhaustive, idea of the absolute and the relative," but also "a spiritual activity that is contemplative in its nature and effectual as concerns our ultimate destiny." In other words, there must be both "discernment between the Real and the illusory, and a unifying and permanent concentration on the Real." As we have seen, this second, practical dimension of religion requires the practice of Prayer above all, but in a context made possible by Virtue and Beauty.

Now clearly, no traditional religious believer, whatever his faith, is going to disagree with the claim that Revelation and the orthodox tradition which issues from it are essential to salvation. What distinguishes the perennial philosopher, however, is the conviction that Heaven has provided mankind with more than one way to be saved, that there exist several authentic Revelations and traditions. Each of these traditions has been providentially adapted to a particular people, and each includes a doctrine and a method which are fully adequate to the attainment of man's final goal. Just as a perennial flower blossoms year after year, so God has repeatedly revealed Himself to man. Outwardly or exoterically—at the level of forms—these religions are different, even incompatible, but inwardly or esoterically they lead in the end to the same conclusion: to a Reality which is necessarily beyond all forms and limitations. When a teacher like Schuon speaks about the existence of a transcendent unity of religions, the word *transcendent* must accordingly be emphasized. The perennial philosopher is not so blind as to miss the obvious multiplicity of dogmas and rites among the world's religions, and he certainly does not mean to advocate a syncretistic amalgamation of forms for the sake of some immanent union. If there is a unity of the religions, it exists in God alone.

It has been claimed, most unfortunately, that Schuon and the other perennialists have attempted to create a new religion, but nothing could be further from the truth. They insist on the contrary that "no present formulation could surpass the ancient formulations; commentaries can be made on the traditional perspectives, they can be summed up from a particular point of view or expressed according to a particular inspiration, but they cannot be contradicted or replaced." Indeed, "it requires a prodigious lack of spiritual sensibility and of a sense of proportion to take any contemporary thinking, even the best possible, for one of the great providential 'crystallizations' of the *philosophia perennis*." It follows that the integrity or "formal homogeneity" of each religion is to be guarded as a precious gift, and no one has been readier or more able in this defense than Schuon and those of his school.

Several analogies can be used in conveying the perennialist conception of religious unity. The various traditions are sometimes compared to geometrical shapes. Each religion "is to total Truth what a geometrical form is to space. Each fundamental geometrical form— such as the point, the circle, the cross, or the square—is an adequate image of the whole of space, but each excludes the others." The religions can also be understood as so many ways of saying *I*. "Revelation means God has said 'I,' that He has revealed Himself to some human receptacle, to some section of humanity. Every religion therefore presents itself as something absolute, and this is strictly comparable with our empirical subjectivity, the unique, exclusive, and irreplaceable—though logically contradictory—character of the ego." I am not you, and you are not I, but this fact does not prevent me from realizing that you have an inward right to name yourself *I*, just as I do myself. Or again, one may think of the differences among the religions on analogy with different positions in space. "The sun is unique in our solar system, but it is not so in space; we can see other suns, since they are situated in space like ours, but we do not see them as suns. The uniqueness of our sun is belied by the multiplicity of the fixed stars, without thereby ceasing to be valid within the system which is ours under Providence."

Whatever the image, the crucial point to be grasped is that the perennial philosopher fully respects the validity, the integrity, and the saving power of more than one orthodox religious tradition. This results in his following yet another middle course between extremes. On the one hand, he is obliged to criticize the exclusivism of those who identify God with the doctrines of their own religion alone. Such people fail to understand that "absolute Truth exists only in depth, not on the surface," at a depth which no one set of dogmas or symbolic forms can exhaust. God, after all, is not only Being, but Beyond-Being—not only Person, but Essence—and while "the Divinity manifests its Personal aspect through each particular Revelation," its "supreme Impersonality" necessarily exceeds all formulation or description, though it is hinted at precisely in "the diversity of the forms of its Word," in the multiplicity of revealed traditions. "In addressing Himself to the individual and to the collectivity—which by definition is made up of individuals—the personal God makes

Himself an individual; that is to say, He creates a religion which is necessarily particular and formalistic and which for that reason could not be universal as regards its form, any more than an individual as such can represent or realize universality. By contrast, the impersonal Divinity does not create religions: the Divine Self confers a universal truth and the corresponding sanctity from within, by illuminating the Intellect and by penetrating into the Heart."

On the other hand, and in view of the opposite extreme, the perennialist must at the same time reject the indiscriminate inclusivism of those who assume that we no longer need the sacred forms bequeathed by a divinely revealed tradition, and who are therefore prepared to ignore those forms or to change them or to mix them with others coming from altogether different, even false, religions—all in the supposed interest of tolerance and religious unity. Schuon insists on the contrary that "Truth does not deny forms from the outside, but transcends them from within," and that "what is mysterious in esoterism is its dimension of depth, its particular developments, and its practical consequences, but not its starting points, which coincide with the fundamental symbols of the religion in question." With this in mind, the perennial philosophers reserve some of their strongest criticisms for those who want to compromise or sacrifice traditional dogmas in order to avoid causing offense and simply for the sake of getting along with each other. "We are as far as can be from approving a gratuitous and sentimentalist 'ecumenism,' which does not distinguish between truth and error and which results in religious indifference and the cult of man." The exclusivism of the most partisan of exoteric believers, firmly convinced that the adherents of other traditions are all bound for hell, is much to be preferred. It is "infinitely closer" to the Truth than "the mental and sentimental universalism of a profane despiser of 'separatist dogmas.'" The perennialist teaches us to be objective and impartial when dealing with men who practice other orthodox religions, and not to permit the intervention of our subjective attachments or personal and temperamental preferences. But he also knows that "objectivity with regard to the perspectives and spiritual ways of other peoples is only too often the result of philosophic indifferentism or sentimental universalism and in such a case there is no reason to pay it homage; indeed one may well ask if objectivity, in the full sense of the word, is in question here. The Christian saint who fights the Moslems is closer to Islamic sanctity than the philosopher who accepts everything and practices nothing."

Let me repeat that a comprehensive treatment of the perennialist perspective on the world's religions is no part of my aim in this short Epilogue. That would demand another book altogether, one in which Schuon's extensive writings on religious doctrine and symbolism were given as full and fair a hearing as his spiritual works have been afforded here. Even supposing, however, that such a study were conducted, the question would no doubt still arise as to what difference it makes. Perhaps you are prepared to accept the idea, for the sake of the argument if nothing else, that there may be more than one saving religion. And yet you may still be wondering what would be gained by this admission. If the unity of the great religions is to be realized only at a level where it will no longer be an issue, then what exactly is the point in proclaiming that unity, especially if it risks being confused in some quarters with relativism or syncretism? A man needs to follow only one tradition to be saved. Why open this Pandora's box? I have found that some people, while not actually rejecting the perennial philosophy as such or in principle, nevertheless for these reasons find it to be an unnecessary speculative luxury, and perhaps you are one of them. Perhaps you would also like to know what the point is.

Three answers can be given. The first and most important for Schuon is that "there is no right superior to that of the Truth." If it is the case that all authentic traditions are so many radii connecting man to the Divine Center, then one should be prepared to say so, however inconvenient or uncomfortable this admission might prove. We have been told that "to be perfectly objective is to die a little," but "there are different ways of dying and differing degrees of death, and the death which does away with religious prejudice—to the extent that the information permits it, and provided it be in the name of that which constitutes the very essence of religion—this assuredly is by no means the least of deaths, though it certainly is the least well known." You will remember our definitions of humility and charity. Humility is treating oneself as another, and charity is treating the other as oneself, in both cases in strict conformity with Truth. What this means in the present case is a willingness to recognize that one's own religion is not alone in claiming to be the way, the truth, and the life. Such a claim is part of the very essence of every authentic Revelation inasmuch as God, who is unique, is its author. Once more we are asked to take into account the two dimensions of the Divine Reality. God is the Absolute. Even on the level of Being or Person, He is absolute in relation to the world and man, and whenever He speaks, it must be with an absolute authority. And yet God is also the Infinite. He is utterly beyond all conceivable limits, and this infinity or plenitude gives rise to a diversity of Revelations—each of them necessarily absolute for those who follow it.

A second response has to do with the present state of the world. As we all know, the boundaries which existed historically between traditional religious civilizations have been all but destroyed. People from many faiths now live and work side by side, with the result that a "narrowly literal belief," which was "still spiritually feasible within a closed system knowing nothing of other traditional worlds," is now "untenable and dangerous in a universe where everything meets and interpenetrates." Our times are such that religious chauvinism or exclusivism is "hard put to hold its own, and whether it likes it or not, has need of certain esoteric elements, without which it runs the risk of exposing itself to errors of a much more questionable kind than *gnosis*." The aim of the present book has been to introduce you to some of these elements, elements that the perennial philosophy is meant to provide—in a way that is "neither fragmentary nor compromised in advance by a denominational bias." By looking along each of the traditional worlds toward the central principles expressed in their doctrines and symbols, the perennialist hopes to assist in guarding those worlds against the skepticism and relativism which inevitably follow the mutual anathemas of religious exclusivists. "Confessional dissensions provoke with good reason doubts and reactions," and the perennial philosophy is presented in part in order "to allow those who have lost their faith to recover the capacity to believe in God, and all the graces that result from it." For "he who does not know how to discern the Truth in every mental form that contains it," and who has been confronted by authentic traditional forms different from his own, "runs the risk of losing the whole Truth contained in some particular form." Certain men will lose their faith altogether, but even those who do not will in self-defense come to cling more and more closely to the bare letter of their religion, to what makes it different from all the others, but at the same time to something which is but a means and not the end of their way.

A final reason to take the perennial philosophy seriously is closely connected to the importance of protecting or guarding faith. The issue in this case, however, is not so much the unprecedented contact between the different religions in our time as it is the timeless fact that men themselves have different spiritual temperaments. We have touched on such differences at several points before, of course. Here I have in mind two basic kinds of people. On the one hand, there are those who can follow no tradition wholeheartedly, or who at least say they cannot, unless they believe that it alone is true. In general, people who take this position tend to have a temperament predisposing them either to the way of good works or to the way of devotion, though one must be careful not to set limits on something as subtle as the human soul. Whatever the temperament, this reaction to the perennial philosophy is a common one. The primary cause for concern in such cases is that perennialist teaching seems to have the effect of demoting or relativizing the religions, and of course one's own in particular. It is seen as a kind of philosophical elitism, which prevents the religious believer from following a given tradition with complete sincerity.

I hope that our meditations will have shown how misplaced is this concern and how unfounded this criticism. Let me say at once, however, that if this is your reaction, too—if you remain unpersuaded that there is a transcendent unity of religions, or if you believe that such a claim compromises our ability to adhere to a particular tradition—then the best advice would be to set the idea aside, and to concentrate instead on the Truth, the Virtue, and the Beauty of your own religion while diligently following its instructions on Prayer. For the last thing that Schuon wants is to distract us from fidelity to a single faith. Take from these pages what makes sense, and leave it at that.

I would be very happy to leave it there myself, confining my advice to Christian terms, were it not that there is a second kind of man, and I do not think that we can in good conscience simply pretend he does not exist. This is the person, usually having a jnanic temperament, who takes just the opposite view from the first, who finds himself unable to follow a spiritual path until he is sure that it is not the only valid expression of Truth. Where the first can believe in no religion unless he thinks that it alone is correct, the second can believe in no religion unless he has been assured that other religions might be true and efficacious as well. "The human individual has one great concern that exceeds all others: to save his soul. To do this, he must adhere to a religion, and to be able to adhere to it, he must believe in it. But since with the best will in the world, one can believe only what is credible, the man who knows to a sufficient degree two or more religions, and in addition has some imagination, may feel himself prevented from adhering to one of them by the fact that it presents itself dogmatically as the only legitimate and the only saving religion—that it presents itself, that is to say, with an absolute exigency, and possibly without offering in its characteristic formulation certain convincing and appeasing elements that one may have found in other religions."

Much as it may amaze or even dismay the exclusivist, there really are people in this second category, those for whom authentic *gnosis* has been a necessary condition for entering a given religious framework. I know of several men and women, including both clergy and monastics, who have entered my own Orthodox Christian tradition only through a door that was first opened by Schuon and the other perennial philosophers. Their knowledge of other religions and their acquaintance with the people who follow them have made it impossible for them to accept the claim that one tradition alone has a monopoly on saving Truth. They do not doubt that salvation comes only through Christ, the Divine *Logos*. But what this means for them is that "all genuine religions are Christian," as certain of the saints have themselves attested. "Every truth is necessarily manifested in terms of Christ and on His model." For such people, "sacred facts are true because they retrace on their own plane the nature of things, and not the other way round: the nature of things is not real or normative because it evokes certain sacred facts." They know that the only absolute is the Absolute. Form as such will therefore remain unconvincing without the interpretations provided by an "integral esoterism."

However strange this may sound to some, and however difficult it may be for religious exoterists to adjust to the existence of so different a perspective, it seems that out of charity they should at the very least not be surprised when they discover this possibility in their midst. On the other hand, those who find themselves attracted to the teaching of Schuon must for their part recognize with equal good will that the perennial philosophy, "the affirmation of the spiritual equivalence of the great revelations," is in no way obligatory for salvation. It could never become "the basis of a system, still less of a method," and should therefore never be allowed to serve as a substitute for an orthodox tradition. For to repeat one of our most important points one final time: the full fruits of Truth, Virtue, Beauty, and Prayer can be realized only within the sacramental context of a single living faith.

SOURCES OF QUOTATIONS

Quotations are identified by the number of the page on which they appear in this book and by the first few words quoted. When two or more passages from the same source closely follow each other, the opening words of the first quotation and the concluding words of the last quotation are together used for identification. Abbreviations refer to the Bibliography of Works by Frithjof Schuon (see below, pages 217–18).

PREFACE

INTRODUCTION

TRUTH

29   In properly intellectual EP 17; mind and body GD 79; irresist-
        ibly to turn GD 66; principial . . . intellection EP 17

30   coincides GD 24; in the Intellect SW 15; all possible knowl-
        edge LT 71; universal faculty GD 80; not in the thinking FA 5;
        static and innate LA 69; the Intellect is in SW 82; the Intellect
        is a LA 93

30–31   uncreated . . . human microcosm SW 81

31   say that there is UT

33   *In metaphysics* GD 60; these perspectives SW 4

35–36   the Transcendent HC 127

36   necessary . . . not be SM 7; The indispensable EP 169; the most
        direct GD 65; All other distinctions SM 7; the supra-ontological
        GD 75

37   Beyond-Being SW 13; There cannot be SW 16; key notion SM
        121; the word 'God' SP 111

38   Just as Being SW 126

38–39   We may thus distinguish HC 142

39   things are in God LT 61; Metaphysical knowledge . . . incommu-
        nicable SW 19

41   *If there are men* SP 166–67

42   the cosmic play SW 109; the fact that SW 64; In and through
        Being DI 144

43   the 'line of demarcation' GD 81; no common measure . . . veil
        itself SW 69; both absolute . . . that can be DH 44; Divine
        Reality FA 54

44   nothingness is the FA 59; All-Possibility SP 108; the
        infinitude GD 60; nothingness . . . effects HC 106; transforms
        water GD 95; but it is nonetheless SW 133; the quite indirect
        FA 54; impossible in the Absolute GD 60–61; it is necessary
        that GD 60–61

44–45   In a certain sense SP 108

45   the world . . . and false SW 11; Reality has entered SW 133; to
        exist means SP 57; 'Evil' is none SW 133

46   those privative FA 58; the root of all evil SW 99; in such
        measure GD 74; Assuredly it can be said SM 16; A mountain
        GD 57

47   *God has opened* PW 56; spend a whole LT 202; fixation of . . . no
        end LT 202

VIRTUE

oclastic hands LT 17; the accident EP 105; we necessarily SM 202; no value . . . for themselves SM 203

66   anonymity of SM 201ff; only our faults SM 204; *gnosis* objectifies . . . the agent SW 147–48; That alone SW 117–18; goes right . . . nature of things SP 196; rooted in existence SP 199; the desire . . . be perfect PW 62

67   *Christ was humiliated* GD 112; able to assume GD 43; Intrinsic Virtue GD 43

68   Every spiritual SP 159; Man cannot become LT 209; the effacing of . . . *gnosis* SP 183; the three great SP 175

69   It is illogical . . . every vice SP 200

70   the conviction of . . . a nothingness SP 201; does not admit . . . an affectation SP 201; surpasses every other GD 111; a voluntarist and SM 209; an obligatory *mea culpa* PM 55; overlook the fact . . . heavenly Paradises PM 30–31; one would like RH 47

71   The fear of God . . . cannot escape SP 217; pride is SM 207; that 'something' SP 206; no man can reach SM 190; ascesis is an SP 148; Since evil SM 215; must be manifested GD 47

72   the cause of EP 148; nothing but collective LA 94; The cosmic possibility EP 148

73   *When man places* SW 94

74   one must know GD 45–46

74–75 In the human SM 194

75   Emotion or sentiment SM 192; emotivity manifests SM 190; necessarily confer SM 194; True knowledge SP 143

75–76 metaphysics is . . . his intelligence GD 42

76   Charity is in SW 93; the busy activity . . . and good GD 46; to rid the soul SW 120

76–77 Since it is SW 95

77   this is merely . . . 'dehumanized' GD 46; a poison which SW 119; while wanting SW 119; In the final analysis SW 119; He who is capable PM 79

78   To love creatures SW 94; the potentiality SP 24; charity starts . . . image of God SP 24; charity or 'compassion' SM 205

79   goodness due to EP 108; There is a hatred PM 7; just contempt EP 118–119; this is an eremitical EP 119; In a spiritual SM 191; the fulminations SM 205

79–80 In the last analysis SP 165

BEAUTY

a sexual being ... vital space HC 6–7; Man stabilizes ... the sun EP 139

120   Man expresses knowledge SW 79; its vertical lines ... crystallization SW 79; the profanation SW 76–77

121   the theophanic quality DH 92; outward Beauty SM 6

123   *This is the mission* HC 30

124   Nothing can be TU 76; conveys transcendent ... of Silence CR 65; there is in the sacred DH 104; nothing is able TU 76; takes into consideration CR 82; there are relativities CR 82; the extreme limit ... surrealism TU 77

125   an adequation ... sacred transmits DH 103; in order that spiritual ... oppose them SP 31; direct and existential SP 33

126   originate first TU 67; transmission of intellectual TU 63; a direct aid CR 66; authentic and normative CR 75; rules that apply TU 62; An art is sacred CR 65; nobility of content CR 77; at very different ... inward in it CR 67; exactness CR 77; symbolism is a ... termed scientific PM 76

126–127   The science GD 92

127   the multiform Beauty SP 33; the crystallization SP 33; what is exteriorized SP 33; Music is interiorized PW 68

128   the discipline TU 67; there must be ... really is TU 71; red excites SP 43; a literal copy HC 30; man must imitate TU 78

129   operates by abstraction HC 30; intelligent observation CR 75

129–130   Thus the icon TU 73

131   *Since Beauty* UT

132   every formal element ... can be avoided UT

133   Exiled on earth EP 196; In nature, each EP 108; the ancient hermits ... softness GD 40; it is in the midst LA 84; the manner of HC 40

133–134   The sense of ... Center DH 105

134   the heart PW 35; It is in the nature EP 205; it favors SW 128; Prior to dress ... happy, calm UT

135   habitation must UT; a base and quantitative CR 79; Every element ... conformity with it EP 180; one must know GD 45–46

136   all the narrations ... to be 'adult' HC 29–30

136–137   we owe it to others ... sanctify himself EP 110

154   fragmenting of the soul . . . Life and Love SW 150; the congenital confusion SW 151; separative illusion SW 152; when man
interiorizes PW 67

155   draws us along . . . at every moment UT; an almost ungraspable . . . already eternal SW 145; it is not Prayer SW
145

156   contribute towards . . . 'Platonic recollection' DH 106; Meditation acts SW 124; it is a precious SW 124

157   the result of persevering UT; bodily substance . . . life and
movement HC 143; symbolic gestures HC 144; can be vehicles
HC 143

157–158   Man is like a tree . . . 'holy silence' HC 143

158   the visual image . . . region of the forehead HC 144; the support
of an existential HC 143; evocative sounds . . . liturgies offer
echoes HC 144; the possibility . . . our existence LA 63; All
great spiritual SW 157; without grace man SP 83; even the
most penetrating LT 204

159   God resides . . . theomorphic Intellect LA 67; the equal and
simultaneous LA 67–68; we can do nothing LA 68; absolute
gratuitousness SP 149; replacing God SP 139; 'mechanical'
factors . . . 'technical' utility SP 139–140; method is itself SP
149; contradictory to speak SP 149

160   natural mysticism SP 149; man always remains SP 93; grace
and method . . . single reality SP 149; active in concentration . . .
distractions SP 93

161   *The man who is chased* EP 170

162   feverishly straining . . . stand before God PW 40

162–163   Wishing to be alone . . . being loved by God PW 77

163   powers or other UT; gift of miracles EP 170; For too many
men SM 218

164   a perfectly worldly SM 218; The desire not to PW 79; on earth
man SM 218; result from our . . . worldly chaff PW 79; all individual interest . . . tangible results UT; inward joys . . . Divine
mysteries PW 63; subtle worldliness PW 78; Instead of
being . . . conjectural UT

165   when a man experiences . . . what we are PW 38; it is as if one
were . . . straight ahead SM 216; If in fact we are saints UT; the
wind which blows SP 139

165–166   As regards concentration EP 170

EPILOGUE

BIBLIOGRAPHY OF WORKS
BY FRITHJOF SCHUON

Titles are listed in the alphabetical order of their abbreviations, as used in the Sources of Quotations.

CI   *Christianity / Islam: Essays on Esoteric Ecumenicism.* Trans. Gustavo Polit. Bloomington, Ind.: World Wisdom Books, 1985.

CR   *Castes and Races.* Trans. Marco Pallis and Macleod Matheson. London: Perennial Books, 1982.

DH   *From the Divine to the Human: Survey of Metaphysics and Epistemology.* Trans. Gustavo Polit and Deborah Lambert. Bloomington, Ind.: World Wisdom Books, 1982.

DI   *Dimensions of Islam.* Trans. P. N. Townsend. London: Allen and Unwin, 1969.

EH   *The Eye of the Heart.* Bloomington, Ind.: World Wisdom Books, 1997.

EP   *Esoterism as Principle and as Way.* Trans. William Stoddart. London: Perennial Books, 1981.

FA   *In the Face of the Absolute.* Bloomington, Ind.: World Wisdom Books, 1989.

FS   *The Feathered Sun: Plains Indians in Art and Philosophy.* Bloomington, Ind.: World Wisdom Books, 1990.

GD   *Gnosis: Divine Wisdom.* Trans. G. E. H. Palmer. London: Perennial Books, 1990.

HC   *To Have a Center.* Bloomington, Ind.: World Wisdom Books, 1990.

IP   *Islam and the Perennial Philosophy.* Trans. J. Peter Hobson. London: World of Islam Festival Publishing Company, 1976.

LA   *Light on the Ancient Worlds*. Trans. Lord Northbourne. Bloomington, Ind.: World Wisdom Books, 1984.

LS   *Language of the Self*. Trans. Marco Pallis and Macleod Matheson. Madras: Ganesh, 1959.

LT   *Logic and Transcendence*. Trans. Peter N. Townsend. London: Perennial Books, 1984.

PM   *The Play of Masks*. Bloomington, Ind.: World Wisdom Books, 1992.

PW   *Echoes of Perennial Wisdom*. Bloomington, Ind.: World Wisdom Books, 1992.

RD   *Road to the Heart*. Bloomington, Ind.: World Wisdom Books, 1995.

RH   *Roots of the Human Condition*. Bloomington, Ind.: World Wisdom Books, 1991.

SM   *Survey of Metaphysics and Esoterism*. Trans. Gustavo Polit. Bloomington, Ind.: World Wisdom Books, 1986.

SP   *Spiritual Perspectives and Human Facts*. Trans. P. N. Townsend. London: Perennial Books, 1987.

SV   *Sufism: Veil and Quintessence*. Trans. William Stoddart. Bloomington, Ind.: World Wisdom Books, 1981.

SW   *Stations of Wisdom*. Bloomington, Ind.: World Wisdom Books, 1995.

TB   *Treasures of Buddhism*. Bloomington, Ind.: World Wisdom Books, 1993.

TM   *The Transfiguration of Man*. Bloomington, Ind.: World Wisdom Books, 1995.

TU   *The Transcendent Unity of Religions*. London: The Theosophical Publishing House, 1984.

UI   *Understanding Islam*. Bloomington, Ind.: World Wisdom Books, 1994.

UT   Unpublished texts and letters

SUGGESTED READING

In addition to the works of Schuon listed in the Bibliography, the following books on the perennial philosophy are also recommended.

Titus Burckhardt, *Alchemy: Science of the Cosmos, Science of the Soul*, trans. William Stoddart (Shaftesbury, Dorset: Element Books, 1986).

———, *Mirror of the Intellect: Essays on Traditional Science and Sacred Art*, trans. William Stoddart (Albany: State University of New York Press, 1987).

———, *Sacred Art in East and West: Principles and Methods*, trans. Lord Northbourne (London: Perennial Books, 1967).

Ananda K. Coomaraswamy, *Coomaraswamy 1: Selected Papers: Traditional Art and Symbolism*, ed. Roger Lipsey (Princeton, N.J.: Princeton University Press, 1977).

———, *Coomaraswamy 2: Selected Papers: Metaphysics*, ed. Roger Lipsey (Princeton, N.J.: Princeton University Press, 1977).

———, *What is Civilisation?* (Great Barrington, Mass.: Lindisfarne Press, 1989).

René Guénon, *The Crisis of the Modern World*, trans. Marco Pallis and Richard Nicholson (London: Luzac, 1975).

———, *Fundamental Symbols: The Universal Language of Sacred Science*, trans. Alvin Moore, Jr., ed. Martin Lings (Cambridge: Quinta Essentia, 1995).

———, *The Reign of Quantity and the Signs of the Times*, trans. Lord Northbourne (London: Luzac, 1953).

Martin Lings, *Ancient Beliefs and Modern Superstitions* (Cambridge: Quinta Essentia, 1991).

Seyyed Hossein Nasr, ed., *The Essential Writings of Frithjof Schuon* (Rockport, Mass.: Element Books, 1991).

———, *Knowledge and the Sacred* (Albany: State University of New York Press, 1989).

Jacob Needleman, ed., *The Sword of Gnosis: Metaphysics, Cosmology, Tradition, Symbolism* (London: Arkana, 1986).

Whitall N. Perry, ed., *A Treasury of Traditional Wisdom* (London: Perennial Books, 1981).

Index

221